TEEN RIGHTS AND FREEDOMS

Custody and Divorce

Teen Rights and Freedoms

Custody and Divorce

Roman Espejo
Book Editor

GREENHAVEN PRESS
A part of Gale, Cengage Learning

Detroit • New York • San Francisco • New Haven, Conn • Waterville, Maine • London

Elizabeth Des Chenes, *Director, Publishing Solutions*

For more information, contact:
Greenhaven Press
27500 Drake Rd.
Farmington Hills, MI 48331-3535
Or you can visit our Internet site at gale.cengage.com.

Articles in Greenhaven Press anthologies are often edited for length to meet page requirements. In addition, original titles of these works are changed to clearly present the main thesis and to explicitly indicate the author's opinion. Every effort is made to ensure the Greenhaven Press accurately reflects the original intent of the authors. Every effort has been made to trace the owners of copyrighted material.

LIBRARY OF CONGRESS CATALOGING-IN-PUBLICATION DATA

Custody and divorce / Roman Espejo, book editor.
pages cm. -- (Teen rights and freedoms)
Includes bibliographical references and index.
ISBN 978-0-7377-6400-0 (hardcover)
1. Divorce--United States--Juvenile literature. 2. Custody of children--United States--Juvenile literature. 3. Parent and teenager--United States--Juvenile literature. 4. Teenagers--Legal status, laws, etc.--United States--Juvenile literature.
I. Espejo, Roman, 1977-
HQ834.C87 2013
346.01'730973--dc23

2012045147

Printed in the United States of America
1 2 3 4 5 6 7 17 16 15 14 13

Contents

Foreword

> *"In the truest sense freedom cannot be bestowed, it must be achieved."*
>
> *Franklin D. Roosevelt, September 16, 1936*

The notion of children and teens having rights is a relatively recent development. Early in American history, the head of the household—nearly always the father—exercised complete control over the children in the family. Children were legally considered to be the property of their parents. Over time, this view changed, as society began to acknowledge that children have rights independent of their parents, and that the law should protect young people from exploitation. By the early twentieth century, more and more social reformers focused on the welfare of children, and over the ensuing decades advocates worked to protect them from harm in the workplace, to secure public education for all, and to guarantee fair treatment for youths in the criminal justice system. Throughout the twentieth century, rights for children and teens—and restrictions on those rights—were established by Congress and reinforced by the courts. Today's courts are still defining and clarifying the rights and freedoms of young people, sometimes expanding those rights and sometimes limiting them. Some teen rights are outside the scope of public law and remain in the realm of the family, while still others are determined by school policies.

Each volume in the Teen Rights and Freedoms series focuses on a different right or freedom and offers an anthology of key essays and articles on that right or freedom and the responsibilities that come with it. Material within each volume is drawn from a diverse selection of primary and secondary sources—journals, magazines, newspapers, nonfiction books, organization newsletters, position papers, speeches, and government documents, with a particular emphasis on Supreme Court and lower court decisions. Volumes also include first-person narratives from young people and others involved in teen rights issues, such as parents and educators. The material is selected and arranged to highlight all the major social and legal controversies relating to the right or freedom under discussion. Each selection is preceded by an introduction that provides context and background. In many cases, the essays point to the difference between adult and teen rights, and why this difference exists.

Many of the volumes cover rights guaranteed under the Bill of Rights and how these rights are interpreted and protected in regard to children and teens, including freedom of speech, freedom of the press, due process, and religious rights. The scope of the series also encompasses rights or freedoms, whether real or perceived, relating to the school environment, such as electronic devices, dress, Internet policies, and privacy. Some volumes focus on the home environment, including topics such as parental control and sexuality.

Numerous features are included in each volume of Teen Rights and Freedoms:

- An annotated **table of contents** provides a brief summary of each essay in the volume and highlights court decisions and personal narratives.
- An **introduction** specific to the volume topic gives context for the right or freedom and its impact on daily life.
- A brief **chronology** offers important dates associated with the right or freedom, including landmark court cases.
- **Primary sources**—including personal narratives and court decisions—are among the varied selections in the anthology.
- **Illustrations**—including photographs, charts, graphs, tables, statistics, and maps—are closely tied to the text and chosen to help readers understand key points or concepts.

- An annotated list of **organizations to contact** presents sources of additional information on the topic.
- A **for further reading** section offers a bibliography of books, periodical articles, and Internet sources for further research.
- A comprehensive subject **index** provides access to key people, places, events, and subjects cited in the text.

Each volume of Teen Rights and Freedoms delves deeply into the issues most relevant to the lives of teens: their own rights, freedoms, and responsibilities. With the help of this series, students and other readers can explore from many angles the evolution and current expression of rights both historic and contemporary.

Introduction

The first recorded divorce in US history took place in 1643, but the principle of the best interests of the child did not emerge until two centuries later. In the colonial period, children were considered to be their father's property under English common law. "The colonial view of children as helping hands gave way to a view that children had interests of their own. Increasingly, these interests became identified with the nurturing mother," explains Mary Ann Mason, a family and child law scholar and author of *From Father's Property to Children's Rights: The History of Child Custody*. This change is reflected in several early court cases. In 1809 a mother was awarded custody of her five-year-old daughter in *Prather v. Prather* after her husband brought another woman into the household in an adulterous relationship. It was the earliest US case that decided against the father. In 1840 a New York court in *Mercein v. People* gave custody of a sick three-year-old girl to her mother. The court declared that she had a natural "attachment for her infant offspring which no other relative will be likely to possess in an equal degree." Nonetheless, custody of the girl was transferred to her father by the state's supreme court two years later. Later in the century, however, the Tender Years Doctrine was widely applied, wherein the courts routinely placed infants, young children, and daughters with mothers to be raised during their "tender years," or under the age of thirteen.

Also in the 1800s, governmental authority over the welfare of children and youths was solidified in a notable court decision. Decided by the Supreme Court of Pennsylvania in 1838, *Ex parte Crouse* affirmed the state's power to remove children from the custody of parents incapable of providing sufficient care, enforcing the doctrine of *parens patriae*, or "the state is the father." Mary Ann Crouse, a Pennsylvania girl, was committed to institutional rehabilitation. Her father argued that it violated her constitutional rights because she was committed without a trial.

The court disagreed, asserting that under *parens patriae* the state was responsible for Crouse's well-being if she could not be cared for by her parents.

During the Progressive Era, which arrived at the turn of the nineteenth century, divorce became widespread in the United States, and the state assumed a greater role in custody and divorce cases. "Legislatures passed strict laws, often buttressed with severe criminal penalties, to compel child support from all fathers, including those who lost their children by judicial decree following divorce," asserts Mason. Parental authority over children under common law, she insists, was essentially broken up by the state. "It made the final decisions on how children should be raised and with whom they should live," Mason continues. "The right to custody, once absolute, could now be severed if the father or mother misused their authority in an abusive or neglectful manner."

The Uniform Marriage and Divorce Act (UMDA) of 1970 further pursued the best interests of children and youth in custody and divorce. The act was conceived by the National Conference of Commissioners on Uniform State Laws to give consistency to marriage and divorce laws. Adopted in various forms across the nation, the UMDA aimed to standardize the best interests of children, including the desires of the parents regarding custody; the desires of the child; and the protection of relationships with parents, siblings, and other individuals important in the child's life. Joan B. Kelly, a clinical psychologist and executive director of the Northern California Mediation Center, expresses a mixed view of this standard. "The best interests standard indicated a willingness on the part of the legal system to consider custody outcomes on a case-by-case basis, rather than adjudicating children as a class or homogeneous grouping," she suggests. Still, Kelly points out, the lack of uniformity in how best interests are defined and weighed—as well as the changing needs of children—is its weakness. "The effect of such unclarity is that attorneys, court workers, and custody evaluators may consider and emphasize different factors or interpret the same concepts, such as continuity or stability, in diametrically opposed ways designed to benefit the parent they represent or favor," she contends.

Numerous divorce and custody cases in the United States have addressed children's and youths' rights. The freedom of older adolescents to choose which parent to live with was upheld in *Guinan v. Guinan*, a 1970 case. In its decision, the South Carolina Supreme Court accounted for the age of the child, seventeen years old at the time, who wished to live with his father. The visitation rights of siblings was denied in *C.R. v. Arthur Z. and Mary Jane Z.*, a 1996 case in which the Pennsylvania Supreme Court ruled that brothers and sisters can only seek visitation if it is specifically protected in their state's custody statutes. More recently, *Troxel v. Granville*, a 2000 case, reached the US Supreme Court, which decided that third parties such as grandparents can only seek visitation if it does not interfere with the parent or parents' constitutional right to raise children as seen fit. The landmark opinion overturned a Washington state statute allowing third-party visitation. *Teen Rights and Freedoms: Custody and Divorce* explores these and other key cases and their impact on the liberties of US youth and families.

Chronology

January 5, 1643 The Quarter Court of Boston, Massachusetts, grants Anne Clarke of the Massachusetts Bay Colony a divorce, the first instance recorded in US history. Her husband, Denis Clarke, left her and their two children for another woman and refused to return to them.

1809 A South Carolina man loses custody of his five-year-old daughter to her mother, in the child's best interests. The case, *Prather v. Prather*, is the first published in US history to rule against fathers, who at that time possessed natural rights over children.

1838 *Ex parte Crouse*, a decision of the Supreme Court of Pennsylvania, establishes the authority of the state to remove children from parents who cannot properly care for them.

1840 In *Mercein v. People*, a New York court awards custody of an ill three-year-old girl to her mother, citing the mother-child attachment and responsibility of the government to protect the welfare of children. Two years later, custody was transferred to her father.

1953 Oklahoma becomes the first state to pass a "no-fault" divorce law, wherein

	the dissolution of a marriage can be sought without proof of misconduct of either spouse.
1970	The Uniform Marriage and Divorce Act defines a standard for the best interests of the child, including his or her wishes regarding custody and relationships with parents, siblings, and other important individuals in the child's life.
July 28, 1970	In *Guinan v. Guinan*, the South Carolina Supreme Court upholds that older adolescents have the right to decide which parent to live with after a divorce.
November 20, 1989	The United Nations Convention on the Rights of the Child is signed, which requires ratifying countries to act in the best interests of children, including their right to be raised by their parents and maintain parental relationships after separation.
June 9, 1992	A Florida court allows a twelve-year-old boy, Gregory Kingsley, to choose to be adopted by his foster parents, terminating the parental rights of his mother.
October 4, 1996	In *C.R. v. Arthur Z. and Mary Jane Z.*, the Supreme Court of Pennsylvania decides that siblings only have visitation rights if they are protected by state custody statutes.

June 5, 2000 The US Supreme Court rules in *Troxel v. Granville* that third-parties cannot seek visitation if it intrudes upon the custodial parent's constitutional right to raise the child as he or she sees fit.

March 29, 2011 In *Traynor n/k/a Dallara v. Traynor*, the Superior Court of New Jersey decides that a child does not have the power to change which parent has custody if the modification does not serve his or her best interests.

VIEWPOINT 1

> *"The ultimate question in each divorce case is 'What is in the child's best interests?'"*

Teens' Rights and Divorce: An Overview

Thomas A. Jacobs

In the following viewpoint, a former judge explains the rights of teens when their parents divorce. He claims that the best interest of the child is the ultimate goal, and he urges teens to make their opinions heard in custody arrangements. However, the author maintains, states follow different laws in giving preference to the child and appointing lawyers or guardians to represent them. After divorce, parents may not interfere with the arrangements; grandparents and stepparents can seek court-ordered visits with teens in numerous states; and teens have the right to financial support from parents until they turn eighteen years old or if they have special needs, he says. Thomas A. Jacobs served as judge pro tem and commissioner for the juvenile and family courts for the Maricopa County Superior Court in Arizona until retiring in 2008. He is the author of What Are My Rights?: Q&A About Teens and the Law.

Excerpted from *What Are My Rights? Q&A About Teens and the Law (Revised and Updated Third Edition)* by Thomas A. Jacobs, JD.

If your parents get a divorce, it doesn't mean that they're no longer your parents, or that they no longer love you. Children are not the cause of their parents' divorce—and they have no reason to feel guilty or blame themselves. If your parents have divorced and you're struggling with feelings of guilt, sadness, or fear, get help so you can work things out in your life. Contact a school counselor, who may recommend that you talk to a therapist or other specialized professional. Or let your mother or father know that the divorce is bothering you, and that you need help dealing with it.

Can your parents force you to go to counseling if you're troubled by divorce (or any other issue)? Yes. They can arrange for the whole family to attend counseling, or individual counseling for one or two of you. Since you have little choice but to go, keep an open mind. It may seem awkward at first, but you'll soon find yourself opening up and feeling better. Relationship issues don't happen overnight, and healing also takes time. Talk with your friends and you'll see that you're not alone in your thoughts, fears, and concerns.

If your parents get a divorce, decisions have to be made that directly affect you. You may have questions: "Do I have to move?" "Will I be separated from my brothers and sisters?" "Will I get to see the parent I don't live with?" A court may help your parents with these decisions, and, depending on your age, you may be asked for your opinion on what you want to happen.

A lawyer may be appointed to represent you if your parents don't agree on visitation issues or where you should live. Tell your lawyer exactly what you feel about these issues and why. This is the only way to be sure that the judge considers your wishes before a decision is made.

The ultimate question in each divorce case is "What is in the child's best interests?" However, the states don't all follow the same laws in determining the answer. Some states give preference to the desires of the child; others don't. Some appoint lawyers or guardians to speak for children; others don't. In most cases, though, the results are the same, since "best interests" remains the goal in all jurisdictions. Both parents are considered in custody disputes about which parent you'll live with. In the past, the law tended to support automatic custody with the mother, but today fathers are often granted custody of their children.

Types of Custody Arrangements

Courts grant either sole custody to one parent, or joint or shared custody to both parents. In a sole custody situation, you'll live with one of your parents and visit the other (for example, on weekends, holidays, and during the summer). If your non-custodial parent lives out of state, you may spend all or part of the summer with that parent. The same is true for your brothers and sisters. Courts try to keep the children in a family together. If siblings are split up, arrangements may be made for frequent contact and visits.

Families often seek professional help, such as counseling with their children, to manage the complicated process of separating due to a divorce. © Bruce Ayers/Getty Images.

Joint or shared custody requires both parents to agree on the living arrangements of the children. It allows both parents to share legal and physical custody of you and your brothers and sisters, with an agreed-upon division of time and responsibilities throughout the year. You may live with your mother during the school year, and with your father during the summer and holidays. Or, if your parents live close by, especially in the same school district, you may alternate weeks or months at each parent's home.

The rule in custody situations should be whatever works out best for all of you. Be sure to speak up and let your parents know how you feel about the arrangements. Whatever is decided, give it a try for a period of time. If you feel strongly one way or the other, tell your parents. It's best to get your feelings out in the open. Speaking up may help change things. You'll also be helping your siblings if they feel the same way but are worried about saying anything.

If you find yourself unable to talk to anyone about divorce and custody worries, pay a visit to your school or public library. You'll find books and pamphlets written especially for children and teens that will help answer some of your questions and concerns. Or look online for similar resources. Check one out—and maybe confide in a friend. . . .

Defining Parental Kidnapping

Kidnapping is defined as knowingly restraining someone with a specific intent to do something. This may be to collect a ransom, use a person as a hostage, or have someone do involuntary work. Other intentions may be to injure a person or to interfere with the operation of an airplane, bus, train, or other form of transportation. Kidnapping may be a felony depending on the circumstances. If someone is convicted of kidnapping, it's not uncommon for that person to receive a jail or prison sentence.

Custodial interference, sometimes called parental kidnapping, happens when one parent keeps a child from the parent who has legal custody. Statistics indicate that over 200,000 children are kidnapped by parents or other family members every year. Specific state and federal laws against parental kidnapping carry stiff sentences for violation.

For example, say the court has placed you in the legal custody of your mother. Your father lives out of state and has holiday visits. After you spend two weeks with your father at Christmas, he decides not to return you to your mother. This is custodial interference and may be prosecuted as a crime.

If your parents agree that you can live with your father, however, they should ask the court to modify the custody order. Courts grant modification requests all the time. The key issue is what's best for you. If there's no risk of abuse or neglect, and the change is to your benefit, it will most likely be approved.

Let your opinion be heard in custody modification situations. Many courts want to know whether you agree with the change of custody. Feel free to write the court a letter. Or you may have the opportunity to go to court and speak with the judge. This is your chance to state your true feelings. If you're hesitant to speak up in your parents' presence, ask to talk to the judge alone. Many judges will allow this. You may be taken to the judge's office with your lawyer or guardian, where you can speak freely. The judge will see that your statements remain confidential.

The point is that you are the most important person in the case. Your opinion matters and should be heard. The results may not be 100 percent to your satisfaction, but speaking up gives you the chance to share your views and to make sure your concerns are taken into account.

Granting Visitation Rights

Visitation is a big issue that gets decided in every divorce case. It starts with your parents. If your mother is given sole custody, your father will probably be granted visitation rights or parenting time. Likewise, if your father is given sole custody, your mother will usually be granted visitation. This means the noncustodial parent will be able to see you on a regular basis, with set times and days. Or it may be more flexible, depending on what your parents agree on. The court will review the terms and, based on what's in your best interests, approve or modify them.

Over the past few years, grandparents and great-grandparents have become active in asserting their requests for visits with grandchildren (and great-grandchildren) whose parents divorce. Many states have passed laws allowing grandparents to seek a court order for visits if they've been denied visitation by the parents. Some states require a minimum period of time to pass (three to six months) before the visits begin—a period where everyone can cool off after the divorce. Other courts require a hearing with an opportunity for parents to oppose grandparent visits if a good reason exists. If visits are granted, the court will usually set forth a schedule that all are required to follow. Each case is unique; there's no specific formula that's followed with identical results each time.

Stepparents may also seek visitation rights. For example, if your mother and stepfather get a divorce, does your former stepfather have any visitation rights? Can you continue to visit the stepparent who is now legally out of the picture? State legislatures are now considering laws addressing parents who find themselves in this situation. Most states, at this time, don't provide stepparents with visitation rights. Some courts, however, will look at the whole picture, including how long the stepparent has been involved in your life, your opinion about visitation, and any other relevant factors. Courts have granted former stepparents visitation with their stepchildren. Again, the bottom line is what's best for you.

The Issue of Child Support

Child support is a hot issue. Headlines scream "Deadbeat Dad Jailed," and names of nonpaying parents are displayed on billboards and wanted posters. Law enforcement officials plan sting operations and holiday arrests.

2009 Marriage and Divorce Rates in the United States

- Number of marriages: 2,077,000
- Marriage rate: 6.8 per 1,000 total population
- Divorce rate: 3.4 per 1,000 population (44 states and D.C. reporting)

Centers for Disease Control and Prevention, "Births, Marriages, Divorces, and Deaths: Provisional Data for 2009," National Vital Statistics Reports, *vol. 58, no. 25, August 27, 2010.*

What's it all about? Why are fathers going to jail? What if mothers miss support payments? Can they be locked up?

First, all parents have a legal duty and obligation to support their children. This includes divorced parents and those who never married. The duty to support a child means providing financial assistance to the custodial parent for the basic necessities of life—food, shelter, clothing, medical expenses, and education. The obligation may apply to either parent—mother or father. The court looks at the whole family situation, including both parents' earnings, standards of living, and debts, and the ages and needs of the children. Guidelines exist to help the court arrive at a fair child support figure. Once the amount is determined, the court makes an order and payments are scheduled to begin, usually on a monthly basis.

As children get older, support payments may be increased as the children's needs change and the cost of living rises. If a parent misses a payment or is occasionally late in paying, any dispute will probably be resolved without going back to court. However, if no payments are made, this becomes a serious matter.

Nationwide, courts and law enforcement agencies have cracked down on parents who are behind in their payments. Why? In part, because taxpayers pay millions of dollars for families on welfare who aren't being supported by responsible parents.

States are trying various methods to get parents to pay their child support. Some states have gone public with billboards and wanted posters in an effort to embarrass "deadbeat" parents into paying. In Arizona, a parent who falls one month behind in child support payments can have his or her professional license (medical, law, therapist, etc.) or work permit or certificate suspended.

If your parents are divorced, their duty to support you continues until you turn eighteen or are emancipated. Some states require child support to continue after your eighteenth birthday if you're still in high school. Once you graduate or get your Graduate Equivalency Diploma (GED), if you are eighteen or over, the legal obligation to support you may end. A number of states also extend the support obligation beyond eighteen if you're physically or mentally disabled. Your parents may agree at the time of the divorce to cover your college or technical school expenses. This will obviously extend support past your eighteenth birthday, and such an agreement has been determined by the courts to be valid and enforceable.

Even if you're a teenage parent, you still have a duty and obligation to support your child or children. Some states require the parents of a teenage mother or father to assist in the baby's support, but the birth parents, regardless of age, carry the primary responsibility.

Children Can Divorce Their Parents

In 1992, a Florida boy named Gregory K. got a court order terminating his mother's parental rights and giving him the legal right to become part of a new family. His birth father didn't contest the adoption. In effect, Gregory "divorced" his parents.

This case was unusual because it was filed by a child with a lawyer's help. Usually, the state or a child welfare agency files this type of lawsuit on behalf of a child. However, when Gregory was eleven, he decided he wanted to remain in the foster home where he'd lived for nine months. Because he'd been neglected and abused by his parents, Gregory had been in foster care for two years. He hadn't seen his mother in 18 months. He thought she had forgotten about him. His new foster parents wanted to adopt him, and the court determined that this was best for Gregory.

Gregory's case opened the door for a whole new discussion and review of children's rights. Since then, state legislatures and courts across the country have paid closer attention to the reasonable and legitimate demands of minors. The emphasis now is on "permanency" for all children and teenagers in foster care. If kids are unable to return home or be placed with relatives, alternative permanent homes are sought. In appropriate cases, public and private agencies take legal action toward terminating parents' rights.

This doesn't mean that because you don't like being grounded, you can go to court and get new parents. This is a serious decision that's limited in its application. Only in the most extreme situation, and usually as a last resort, will the legal rights of a parent be terminated.

If things are seriously wrong in your family and you have questions or problems that you've been keeping to yourself, find someone you trust and can talk to. A school counselor, teacher, clergy member, or adult friend or family member may be someone you can turn to. Don't let the situation get so out of control that your health and safety are at risk. Community groups or Child Protective Services (CPS) are good resources for assistance.

VIEWPOINT

> *"When parents of teens choose to divorce, they and the court generally want to consider their teens' preferences regarding where and with whom they will live."*

Should Your Adolescent Have a Say?

Michael C. Gottlieb and Jeffrey C. Siegel

In the following viewpoint, two psychologists suggest that parents and the court should consider with whom adolescents prefer to live in divorce arrangements. A child's decision-making ability and judgment should be evaluated by a mediator or specialist if parents cannot accurately assess his or her needs, the authors state. Also, research demonstrates that adolescents benefit from such involvement, the authors maintain, by reducing conflict and giving them more control in divorces. Michael C. Gottlieb is a forensic psychologist and a clinical professor at the University of Texas Health Science Center. Jeffrey C. Siegel is a forensic and clinical psychologist who has conducted child custody evaluations for three decades.

Jim and Joan Jones have decided to divorce. They have two teenagers, Jimmy, 15, and Joanie, 13. Jim and Joan would prefer

Michael C. Gottlieb and Jeffrey C. Siegel, "Should Your Adolescent Have a Say?," *Family Advocate*, vol. 33, no. 1, Summer 2010, p. 16.

to settle their differences amicably; but Joan thinks the children would be better off with her, and Jim feels they should be with him. On one hand, they wonder if the children should decide for themselves, and on the other, whether the children's opinions should be sought at all. They decide to ask their lawyers.

When parents of teens choose to divorce, they and the court generally want to consider their teens' preferences regarding where and with whom they will live and how much time they will spend with the other parent. Furthermore, teens want to have their preference known and feel better when their opinions have been considered.

As a result of extensive research on adolescent decision-making, we now know much more about how they think and how capable they are of making such decisions. Following is a primer on what the research shows. It begins with parenting styles.

Three Kinds of Parenting

The permissive parent attempts to behave in a nonpunitive, accepting, and affirming manner toward the child's impulses, desires, and actions; consults with the child about decisions and gives explanations for family rules; makes few demands for household responsibility and orderly behavior; allows the child to regulate his or her own activities as much as possible; avoids the exercise of control; and does not encourage the child to obey externally defined standards, which are often considered arbitrary.

Children who are raised in such environments are at risk for disrespecting authority and violating rules. Furthermore, permissive parenting contributes to an increased likelihood of adolescent experimentation with drugs and alcohol, participation in minor delinquency, and disengagement from school. In another study, anxiety and depression were higher among adolescents with parents who reported lower levels of behavioral control.

The authoritarian parent attempts to shape, control, and evaluate the behavior and attitudes of the child in accordance with a predetermined and rigid standard of conduct. Authoritarian parents value obedience as a virtue and favor punitive, forceful measures to curb "self-will" at points where the child's actions or beliefs conflict with what the parent thinks is right and proper. Such parents believe in keeping the child in his or her place, restricting autonomy, assigning household responsibilities to inculcate respect for work, discouraging verbal give-and-take, and believe that the child should accept the parents' word for what is right.

Children who are raised by authoritarian parents may have difficulty establishing their own independence as they have little experience in making decisions for themselves.

The authoritative parent attempts to direct the child's activities, but in a rational, issue-oriented manner. Parents encourage verbal give-and-take, share with a child the reasoning behind the rule or restriction, and solicit objections when the child refuses to conform. Both autonomous self-will and disciplined conformity are valued. Such a parent enforces his or her own adult perspective, but recognizes the child's individual interests and special ways. The authoritative parent affirms the child's present qualities, but also sets standards for future conduct.

Research suggests that these children are most likely to thrive as they are allowed decision making within their capability and appropriately established parental limits.

To be more specific, teens who had either authoritative parents or only a mother who was authoritative reported greater well-being than those with no authoritative parent. Similarly, fifth graders of parents who exerted greater external control and provided less guidance had poorer academic achievement that year, and within two years, had greater difficulty with self-motivation. In contrast, when parents supported their children's autonomy, the children had higher academic achievement that year and greater internal motivation in seventh grade.

In a related study, authors found that an authoritative parenting style had a very positive impact on children's self-concept.

Permissive parenting has been found to contribute to higher levels of anxiety, disengagement, and depression among adolescents. © Nancy Ney/Getty Images.

This study suggests that parents remain an important source of guidance for their developing children, even in late adolescence. Similarly, authoritative parenting provided the most significant contribution to children's ability to cope with adversity, regardless of gender and racial differences.

These studies tell us that parents retain influence in adolescents' lives and may do so even in the face of potentially negative peer influence.

Susceptibility to peer pressure in adolescence increases to a peak around age 14, and declines thereafter across all demographic groups. Resistance to peer influences increases between ages 14 and 18 years of age. Middle adolescence is an especially significant period for the development of a capacity to stand up for what one believes and resist the pressures of one's peers to do otherwise.

Parental Influence Continues

Social scientists had assumed that parental influence is sharply curtailed in adolescence, a time during which peers have greater influence and parents have diminishing control. What we have learned is that parents retain notable, albeit more indirect, influence over their teenager's peer relations. For example, specific authoritative parenting practices (e.g., monitoring, encouragement of achievement, joint decision making) are strongly linked with particular adolescent behaviors, such as better academic achievement, lower drug use, and greater self-reliance. In addition, teens do better and feel better about themselves when they know that their authoritative parents accept them for who they are.

In a related study, parents were more inclined to talk with their teens about their personal or emotional welfare, but they were more inclined to punish when teens misbehaved in areas regarding physical safety and in understanding the rights of others. In response, teens reported feeling that doing nothing was not appropriate for parents when issues regarding understanding the rights of others and avoiding harm arose. With regard to personal/emotional welfare, teens viewed talking as appropriate, whereas yelling and punishment were not. Teens were more likely to behave in a positive way when they viewed their parents' responses to their behavior as appropriate and reasonable.

Recognizing the Uniqueness of Adolescence

> On issues as varied as liability for contracts and the weight accorded to teens' preferences in divorce custody disputes, lawmakers have recently taken tentative steps towards recognizing the uniqueness of this development stage. Developmental research underscores the notion that adolescents resemble both children and adults in many ways, depending on the context and circumstances. The developmental realities of adolescence alone will never dictate legal regulation, but developmental research and theory can provide the empirical foundation for policies that promote a healthy and productive transition from childhood to adulthood.
>
> *Jennifer L. Woolard and Elizabeth Scott, in Richard M. Lerner and Laurence Steinberg, eds.,* Handbook of Adolescent Psychology, Contextual Influences on Adolescent Development, Volume 2. *Hoboken, NJ: John Wiley & Sons, 2009.*

Therefore, how parents discipline their teens is less important than the degree to which their children view their responses as appropriate.

So what are the Joneses to do? If we look at only these studies, they tell us that if Jim and Joan have been authoritative parents, accepting their children as individuals, and disciplining them appropriately, chances are greater that their children will make better decision for themselves and benefit from being involved in decision making.

Thinking and Judgment

Adolescents and young adults (generally ages from 13 to 24) take more risks than younger or older individuals, a phenomenon that has puzzled researchers for years. What we've learned is that adolescents' inclination to engage in risky behavior does not appear to be due to irrationality, delusions of invulnerability, or ignorance. Rather, there is a gap in time between puberty, which impels adolescents toward thrill seeking, and the slow maturation of the cognitive control that regulates these impulses. It is this gap that makes adolescence a time of heightened vulnerability for risky behavior.

Recent research on adolescent brain maturation indicates that the systems responsible for logical reasoning and basic information processing (thinking) mature before those responsible for social maturity (judgment). A recent study concluded that it is not wise to make sweeping judgments about the maturity of adolescents relative to adults because the answer depends on the aspects of maturity under consideration. By age 16, adolescents' general thinking abilities are essentially indistinguishable from those of adults, but adolescents' social functioning and decision making, even at age 18, is significantly less mature than that of individuals in their mid-20s.

Widely Ranging Abilities

Socially responsible decision making is significantly more common among young adults than adolescents. This finding challenges the assumption that adolescents and adults are equally competent socially, and, thus, laws and social policies should treat them equally. Instead, the picture is far more complex since adolescents' judgmental abilities range far more widely than we previously had thought. Some adolescents will exhibit more mature decision making than others. Teens who do should be able to have a greater say in custodial decisions than those who are less capable.

This information may place the Joneses in a difficult position if they do not have a clear sense of where their children are developmentally. This is understandable since adolescence is such a moving target. Therefore, Jim and Joan might consider having a child specialist or court-appointed mental health professional talk with the children and provide an initial assessment of their abilities in this regard.

In various studies, teens subjected to more parental hostility than their siblings showed more acting-out behavior, and parental conflict made matters worse. Furthermore, teens who exhibited more behavioral problems than their siblings received more hostile mothering, and, as a result, their younger siblings were also subject to more hostile mothering. Given this situation, when parents divorce, hostile mothering, for example, could easily prompt a teen to want to live with the father, even though such an impulse may not be in the adolescent's best interest.

Along similar lines, marital conflict was associated with lower self-esteem, more acting-out symptoms, and lower academic achievement in children. Children of parents who exerted more psychological control, such as being authoritarian and/or more intrusive, were more likely to be anxious or depressed. On the other hand, parental warmth was associated with children's decreased acting-out behavior and increased self-esteem over time.

If the Jones children speak with a mental health professional, one of the questions that will arise is how have they been reared. Even if it turns out that one or both of them is having some difficulty with their feelings or behavior, this may not be the child's fault. Teens live within the context of a family, and when they have problems, all members of the family should be evaluated to determine the cause of the problem. This assessment should be completed before deciding how much say a child can have. This step is essential since resolving certain family issues may help the adolescent make better decisions for themselves.

One study found that the frequency of parent-child conflict was tied to first-borns' difficulty in transitioning to adolescence, but second-borns experienced no such problems. These findings highlight that all siblings do not have identical problems with their parents as they move into adulthood and that parents may learn from their experiences with older children.

Kids Benefit from Having a Say

Considering teen preferences is difficult because, as noted above, adolescence is a moving target. It is a time of rapid development during which teens experiment and learn about the world as they mature. This period of development brings both opportunities to exercise choice and the consequences of those choices from which parents can often offer little protection. Therefore, understanding how teens make decisions is vital to the discussion. Never uncritically accept what a teen says. Rather, it is important to understand the complexity of the teen's situation and the bases for his or her preferences within a dynamic family situation.

Two Australian articles recently addressed the importance of children's involvement in their parent's divorce. One focused on why children should be heard within the context of mediation when using a child specialist to facilitate the process. One year later, these parents reported a general reduction in conflict and an increase in resolution of subsequent conflicts, and the children agreed. The vast majority of parents stated that their children should have a "say" in where they want to live, but when asked if such preferences should be determinative, only 22 percent of parents felt that it should be, and nearly fifty percent worried that their children might be manipulated in the process.

Seventy percent of all children felt uncomfortable with the process; they wanted to be included, but nearly all said they did not want to have the final say. Children referred to feeling better if they knew what was going on and if they had some control over the situation, rather than being at the "mercy" of their parents' actions and decisions.

The second study made three important points. First, parents who mediated and used a child specialist felt that the feedback they received about their children helped them to reach a consensus on children's needs and to change their behavior toward each other. Second, fathers in this group felt that bringing a child specialist into the process leveled the playing field as it removed mothers from the role of "gate keeper of the truth" about the children. Third, parents' agreements favored stability of residence and improved relationships.

How much say children should have will depend on a number of things, but social science can tell us a good deal. When parents can accurately evaluate their children's needs, they may need little or no decision-making help. But all parents cannot do this, and genuine disagreements may arise. One point that emerges from this research is that if conflict arises, the Joneses would be well-advised to consider hiring a mediator and mental health professional to work out their differences.

Viewpoint 3

> *"I finally have a peaceful and loving family, just not the one I expected."*

A Teen Talks About Separating from Her Abusive Father and Accepting Her Stepfather

Personal Narrative

Anonymous

In the following viewpoint, a California teen discusses how her relationship with her father ended—and a new one began with her stepfather—after her parents divorced. Despite her father's physical and emotional abuse of her mother and brother, the author says that she maintained a relationship with him. However, she explains that her father lashed out in rage when her mother became engaged, and she ceased all contact with him. After her mother remarried, the author claims, she did not accept her stepfather until he proved to be unlike her father and provided a stable home.

Anonymous, "I'm Better Off Without My Dad," *L.A. Youth*, January–February 2012. www.layouth.com.

It's been more than a year since I've talked to my dad. My dad was abusive to my family so I don't want him in my life anymore.

He only spanked me to discipline me when I fought with my brother. But he hit my brother every week. When I was 6, my 5-year-old brother told my dad that he didn't want to go to Bible camp. My dad cursed at him and repeatedly kicked him in the stomach in the church parking lot. My dad didn't hit my mom in front of me, but later my mom told me that he hit her frequently.

I tolerated what my dad did to us because I couldn't do anything about it and he treated me like his favorite. There were also good times with my dad. Some nights, he made me and my brother laugh until we cried by telling us about the time he lost a finger while fixing a machine when he was in the Korean army.

These were the moments that made me feel like my dad could change and be loving. I wanted my family to be happy. But everything I was hoping for didn't happen.

One day when I was 8, my parents were fighting in the kitchen, while I listened to the argument in the living room. I heard my mom say, "I'm going to get a divorce!" and my dad say, "I'll kill you first and then burn your parents' house down!" I was scared, so I started to cry and rock myself back and forth. I heard utensils rattle, someone get slapped and my mom scream. I thought about running to my neighbors for help or calling the police. But I didn't do anything because I feared that the police would take my brother and me away.

Thirty minutes later, my dad came out and stomped into the bedroom, while my mom hurried off to the bathroom. When I caught a glimpse of my mom's face, I saw red puffy eyes from crying and small cuts on her face from where he'd cut her with a knife. I was shocked.

Enough of the Abuse

Not long after that fight, my mom decided to separate from my dad. We went to a domestic violence shelter that was disguised as an apartment. After about a month, we moved to an apartment near my school and my mom's work, even though it was also close to my dad's house.

A few months later, my dad found out where we were living after he spotted us walking near our home. He came to our apartment several times, wanting us to open the door. We moved to another apartment and he found us there, too.

A few weeks later, my dad told my mom in court that he wanted to see me and my brother. We didn't think he would do anything bad to us in public, so my mom allowed him to take me and my brother out to restaurants.

After the second time, my brother stopped going because he never liked my dad. But I went out to eat with my dad throughout elementary and middle school. He was fun unlike my mom. The mood in my home was depressing because my mom stressed over work and having to raise two kids on her own. My dad took me to the mall, the fair and the Huntington Library. My mom just liked to rest at home after work and on the weekends.

But my relationship with my dad was complicated. There were times in the car when out of nowhere, he would yell at me about how my mom was a psycho for ripping the family apart and how it was her fault that he had to drive me home. I felt like he was trying to turn me against my mom. I would scream back, "You're the psycho! You hit us and never appreciated us. That's why we left. Why can't you just accept it?" When we arrived at my house, I would run out of the car, go in my room and cry on my bed.

After our fights, he would always call and promise to take me out to a nice restaurant or give me $200. I would accept his offer and continue to see him. I liked hanging out with my dad because I got to keep both of my parents in my life.

The Emergence of New Relationships

When I was in seventh grade, my dad got remarried. I went to my dad's house every weekend. My stepmom cooked delicious meals. I walked to the library with my 3-year-old stepsister and helped her ride her tricycle.

While I was hanging out with my dad, my mom was going on dates. My mom kept seeing this guy she had gone on a blind date with. I didn't like this guy at all. He was 10 years older than my mom, he smoked and he wasn't much of a talker. One day

Negative Myths About the Impacts of Divorce on Children

- There is no convincing evidence to support the cultural myth that divorce has a negative impact on the involved children or that children of divorce are not as well-adjusted as children of intact marriages. In fact, for some children the divorce can result in a lessening of stress and a freedom from the discord, tensions, and even violence that predated the actual separation or divorce.
- Children of divorce can become model, happy, productive citizens while children of intact marriages can become outrageous criminals. The successful children of divorce are not simply "the exception that proves the rule" any more than the delinquent children of intact marriages are proof that marriage in itself has a toxic influence on child development.
- Having a divorce in one's background is not the ultimate determining factor in adolescent or adult behavior. This is not meant to minimize the stress of discord and divorce on children. But . . . the negative myth about the impact of divorce does not take into account the natural "resiliency" of many children.

Mel Krantzler and Patricia Biondi Krantzler, Moving Beyond Your Parents' Divorce. *New York: McGraw-Hill, 2003.*

when I was in ninth grade, my mom told me that she was going to marry him and that we were going to move to another city closer to his work as soon as school ended. I said, "Stop joking. That's not funny."

But my mom's decision was final. She went out every weekend with her fiancé to look for a house that they could rent. She would occasionally invite him over to our house for dinner. I didn't like eating with him because he never talked and it was weird to have a grown man in our house.

One day, someone broke into my mom's car. Her fiancé skipped work to drive her to her job, took her car to the repair shop and picked her up again. If my mom had still been with my dad, he wouldn't have done anything except scream at her. When my mom's fiancé came over that night, I made him toast shaped like a heart to show my appreciation.

Letting Go of the Past

But still, I didn't want to believe that he was going to be my new dad. One day, I told my mom that she shouldn't marry someone she'd known for less than a year. She replied, "When you get to my age and experience lots of things, you know what's right for you. And I know that he is right for me, you and your brother. If you don't want me to marry, you can just go live with your dad."

Of course I wanted to live with my mom because I knew that my dad was nice only when I was with him. I knew he still had problems with his anger because I would sometimes catch him yelling at my stepsister or my stepmom. Although my mom and I argue sometimes, I love her and appreciate everything she does for me. But, I thought my mom should have let me get to know her fiancé for a long time before making such a life-changing decision.

In my room, I thought about everything I would lose if my mom got married and I moved: a good relationship with my dad and stepfamily, my friends, the city where I'd grown up. I didn't want to let them go.

But one day, my dad and I got into the biggest argument we've ever had and I realized that he would never change. While driving me home from lunch, he kept pressuring me to tell him who the male voice was that he'd heard in the background when he called a few days before. He kept saying, "Your mom has a boyfriend, doesn't she?" I started crying. I didn't want to lie to him anymore. I would always tell him my mom wasn't seeing anyone or it was none of his business when he asked questions like that. My dad said, "It's OK. I'm not mad. I understand how you feel." But a few seconds later, he yelled, "Give me your phone. Call your mom right now. It's her fault that you're crying. She's crazy. Call that f***ing b**** NOW!"

I wanted him to understand the hurt I'd been feeling, but he only cared about himself. He was jealous that my mom was seeing another guy and he wanted to yell at her about it. I yelled back, "Why do you give a s*** if mom's dating someone? You have your own wife! You're crazy, not mom. I hate you!" He said, "If you hate me, why do you want to see me so often?" I said, "I wanted to keep you in my life because I loved you." I had told him how I really felt and he laughed. I got even angrier.

We kept yelling at each other. Once we arrived at my house, I slammed his car door and stormed inside. I cried for two hours in my room and promised myself that I wouldn't talk to him again. I was tired of fighting, making up and repeating the cycle. When my mom came home from work, I told her that I was more than happy to move to another city and she told me I made a good decision. On the first day of summer vacation, we moved 30 miles away.

Throughout the summer, my dad called me but I never picked up the phone. It was really hard not to give in, but I knew that he'd manipulate me to find out where I lived if I met up with him. I didn't want my dad coming to our house and harassing us like he had when we lived in L.A. That would get my stepdad involved and things would get complicated. I don't want to deal with any of that.

Adjusting to a New Family Life

After the wedding in July, my stepdad moved in. I didn't want to live with him. I believed that every man had the potential to be as mean as my dad so I tried to annoy him so he'd get violent; his kindness seemed like an act to win me over. Then, my mom would see that it was like living with my dad all over again and leave him. I'd ask, "Did you go to the market?" and walk away before he finished speaking. I would say, "Hey you," instead of calling him "dad." But he never yelled or hit any of us. He was patient and understanding, so after a year I stopped being a brat. I felt sorry for acting the way I did. When I talked in funny accents and made him laugh my mom told me that she was thankful that I was trying to be nice.

Since my mom comes home late from work, my stepdad cooks for me and my brother. I love the kimchi soup he makes from scratch. When I ask him to drive me somewhere at the last minute, he says, "OK sure." Since my stepdad doesn't yell at little things like my dad used to, I feel like I can ask him or talk to him about anything.

One day, when I was unloading groceries from his car, my voice shook a little as I said, "Dad, do you want me to close the trunk?" It was so awkward to say "dad." But I kept practicing and now it feels normal. I finally have a peaceful and loving family, just not the one I expected.

It's been more than a year since I've talked to my dad. I'm sad that he is not a part of my life anymore. I miss eating dinner with him and going places like we used to. I sometimes wonder what he's doing. I still sometimes cry about not having him in my life anymore. But I know it's better because it creates less heartbreak.

My family isn't perfect. We have minor issues that every family deals with, but not the kind of problems when someone is abusive. I'm grateful for how things turned out.

VIEWPOINT 4

> *"When faced with [the question of religion], the court must weigh the benefits and costs of one parent's First Amendment rights versus the best interests of the child."*

Divorce: Child Custody and Religion

FindLaw

In the following viewpoint, a legal reference website explores court rulings determining what religion children observe if their divorced parents have different religions. Generally, the author claims, the courts attempt to meet the child's best interests and parents' freedom of religion and childrearing. The author adds that state courts usually follow or apply one of three standards in these custody cases. Nonetheless, these standards have resulted in different outcomes in the courts, asserts the author. FindLaw is a website that provides free legal information and online marketing for law firms.

How do courts decide which religion a child should follow when parents of different religions separate?

Deciding whose religion a child should follow after a divorce or separation can often be a difficult and contentious question to answer. Increasingly parents of different faiths marry and have children. When these parents get divorced, it is often up to the courts to decide which religion a child should follow. These types of questions are answered by many courts all across the country with the result that there is not a uniform standard that courts follow when answering this hard question.

Best Interests of the Child or the Rights of Parents?

When courts are asked to answer the question of what religion a child should follow after a separation or divorce, they often balance two competing interests, the best interests of the child, and the rights of the parents. On one side, courts routinely answer questions about what is in the best interests of a child and have become quite proficient with these types of issues. On the other hand, the First Amendment of the United States Constitution protects the parents' freedom of religion as well as their right to raise their child under the religion of their choosing.

Often, in a case where a court must make a decision about the child's religious upbringing, one parent will argue that raising the child under the other parent's religion will put the child's welfare in danger. When faced with this question, the court must weigh the benefits and costs of one parent's First Amendment rights versus the best interests of the child.

Child Custody and Religion Law in Custody Cases

In general, there is not a national standard for cases involving the religious upbringing of a child after a divorce. Because of this, the law varies from state to state. However, most state courts will generally apply one of the following standards when ruling in a child custody and religion case:

- *Actual or substantial harm standard.* When a court follows this standard, the court will restrict a parent's First

Amendment right to raise their child under the religion of their choosing only if that parent's religious practice causes actual or substantial harm to the child.

- *Risk of harm standard.* When a court follows this standard, the court will only restrict a parent's First Amendment right to raise their child under the religion of their choosing if a parent's religious practice may cause harm to the child.
- *No harm standard.* When a court follows this standard, the court does not consider any actual or potential harm to the child. Instead, the parent that has been granted custody of the child gets to choose which religion the child will follow. If the custodial parent objects to the non-custodial parent's wishes for the religion of the child, the court will side with the custodial parent.

Actual or Substantial Harm

Under this standard, a court will only restrict a parent's First Amendment right to raise their child under a religion of their choosing when the other parent can prove that those religious activities cause actual or substantial harm to the child. There are many states that follow this standard including California, Colorado, Florida, Idaho, Indiana, Iowa, Maryland, Massachusetts, Montana, Nebraska, New Jersey, New York, North Dakota, Ohio, Rhode Island, Utah, Vermont, and Washington.

What follows are a list of cases that show how the actual or substantial harm standard was applied to a variety of situations. You should keep in mind that even if you find a case that you think may apply to your situation, if the case did not take place in your state, your state's courts may not apply the law in the same way. Indeed, courts in the same states do not always apply the same law in a uniform manner.

Munoz v. Munoz. This case ruled that exposing children to two different religions does not, in itself, cause harm to the children.

Courts often have the burden of deciding which religion a child will practice after a divorce. © Paul Burns/Getty Images.

In *Munoz v. Munoz*, Washington State's highest court had to decide whether exposing a child to two different religions in itself caused harm to the child. In this case, the divorce court awarded sole custody of the children to the mother, who was Mormon.

After the custody award, the mother asked the court to prevent the father, who was Catholic, from exposing the children to his own faith. However, the mother did not provide any evidence or likely arguments that exposing the children to both the Mormon and Catholic faiths would harm the children, either physically or mentally. Because of this, the Washington State Supreme Court ruled that exposing children to two different religions does not automatically harm the children and decided not to curtail the father's First Amendment rights to raise his children under his faith.

Pater v. Pater. This case ruled that religious customs are not harmful unless proven otherwise.

In *Pater v. Pater*, the Ohio Supreme Court overruled a lower court decision that had switched the custody award from the mother to the father. The lower court had decided that way because the mother, who originally had sole custody, was a Jehovah's Witness and had the children practicing her faith. Under the mother's faith, the children could not celebrate any holidays, be friends with anyone outside of the religion, salute the American flag or sing the national anthem. The lower court decided that this was harmful to the children.

However, the Ohio Supreme Court reversed this decision and took sole custody away from the Catholic father. In doing so, the court ruled that religious customs that diminish a child's social activities are not harmful (even if the customs separate the child from his or her peers or preach against standards of the community), unless it can be proven that the customs directly cause physical or mental harm to the child. Here, the Ohio Supreme Court did not see any evidence of direct physical or mental harm.

Kendall v. Kendall. This cased ruled that physical acts and verbal threats were enough to justify an intervention of a parent's First Amendment rights.

In *Kendall v. Kendall*, the Massachusetts Supreme Court was dealing with a case that involved an Orthodox Jewish mother and a Catholic father. When the couple was first married, they agreed to raise their children under the Jewish faith. After the mother filed for divorce, the father made threats to his son. These threats included the threat to cut off his son's religious clothing unless he tucked them into his pants as well as a threat to cut off his sons "payes" (the curls in the hair that are normally worn by Orthodox Jewish men). In addition, the father told his children that anyone outside of his Catholic faith was damned to go to hell.

The mother challenged the father's First Amendment rights based on testimony from a doctor that the father's threats caused mental and emotional harm to the children. Because of the evidence that was presented, the court prohibited the father from talking to his children about his faith and also banned him from shaving off his son's payes. In addition, the [court] barred him from studying the Bible with his children and praying with them if those activities would tend to get the children to reject the Orthodox Jewish faith or cause emotional distress.

Risk of Harm

There are a few states, including Minnesota, Montana, North Carolina, and Pennsylvania, which follow the risk of harm standard instead of applying the actual or substantial harm standard. Courts that follow the risk of harm standard only require that the parent challenging the other parent's First Amendment right show that there is a risk of harm instead of showing actual or substantial harm.

MacLagan v. Klein. This case ruled on the risk of harm standard.

In *MacLagan v. Klein*, a North Carolina state court was faced with a case where the father of a child wanted to stop the mother from changing their daughter's faith. When the couple was first married, they agreed to raise their children under the father's Jewish faith. When the couple divorced, the mother began

Child-Rearing Rights and Children as Separate Persons

Arguably, it is rational of parents, within their scheme of values, to demand child-rearing rights if they believe themselves bound by their faith to raise their children in a way that is inconsistent with the children's temporal interests. Within their conception of the good, spiritual aims may conflict with and outweigh some worldly aims. In addition, some parents, whether religious or not, may derive some immediate satisfaction from enjoying unfettered discretion to direct their child's life in the way they see fit.

However, even if rights to control a child's life in ways inimical to the child's temporal interests would further some interests of the parents, these rights may not serve other, long-term parental interests. For example, not having such rights might better lead parents to recognize their children as separate persons whose well-being is also the concern of other people. It might lead parents to consider that their own views of what is right for their children may not be the same as what the children would choose for themselves if able to do so.

James G. Dwyer, "Parents' Religion and Children's Welfare: Debunking the Doctrine of Parents' Rights," California Law Review, *vol. 82, no. 6, December 1994.*

bringing their daughter to a Methodist church. The father did not agree with this decision and asked the court to allow him to have full control of his daughter's religious upbringing. Applying the risk of harm standard, the court found that the daughter had identified herself with the Jewish faith since the age of three and that exposing her to the Methodist faith may cause her emotional harm. Because of this, the court agreed with the father and granted him sole control over his daughter's religious education.

You may have noticed the big difference between the *MacLagan* case and the *Munoz* case. The two cases had very similar facts that the courts looked at, but came out with two very different outcomes. The difference in outcomes is based on the fact that the two courts applied very different standards to their decision making process.

No Harm

There are a few states, including Arkansas and Wisconsin, which do not look at any harms, whether real or a risk, to children and instead defer to the parent with custody of the child. In general, in states that follow the no harm standard, the parent that has sole legal custody over the child has the sole right to decide on the religious education of the child. If a dispute arises between the custodial parent and the non-custodial parent, the court will generally decide to side with the custodial parent. In general, the courts that decide this way that the decision is in the best interests of the child and that any restrictions on the non-custodial parent's First Amendment rights is small because the only time the rights are curtailed is when the parent is with the child.

If both parents have been granted legal custody of the child, both parents are generally allowed to give the child their own religious education.

Johns v. Johns. The court ruled that the parent with legal custody gets to decide.

In *Johns v. Johns*, an Arkansas state court agreed with the mother who had both legal and physical custody of the children. In this case, the court was faced with a problem where the mother of the children refused to allow the father his visitation time because he did not take the kids to church or Sunday school when he was supposed to. The father challenged this action, but the mother prevailed in court because she was the custodial parent and the court agreed with her and ordered that the father must take the children to church and Sunday school.

Zummo v. Zummo. The court ruled that joint legal custody can mean two religions.

In *Zummo v. Zummo*, the court was faced with a problem where both parents shared legal custody of the children but disagreed on which religious upbringing their children should take part in. To put a stop to the problem, the court ordered that the father needs to take his children to Jewish services (the mother's religion), but was also allowed to bring his children to Catholic services as well (his religion). The court rationalized that because both parents shared legal custody, they both had the right to provide their children with their own religion's education.

Some States Can Use More than One Standard

You should be aware that in some states, like Montana and Pennsylvania, courts often use different standards. For instance, one court in Montana could use the actual or substantial harm standard while another court in the same building may decide to apply the risk of harm or no harm standard.

Child Custody and Religion—Parenting Agreements

Courts will often take parenting agreements into account in their decisions if parents have made some sort of written or oral parenting agreement where they decide how to [handle] a child's religions upbringing. However, you should keep in mind that if you and your spouse have not followed the agreement, you should not expect the court to give it too much weight. As well, many courts will not give weight to any agreements that take into account which religion a child will follow in the event that the parents separate or divorce. Here are some of the reasons that courts give:

The agreement is not detailed enough. Generally speaking, many parents do not think a parenting agreement regarding children and religion is very important and because of this they are often informal and vague. As an example, most agreements do not take into account the degree of religious education that a child will receive (such as whether or not the child will attend Sunday school or how often the child will attend religious services) and merely specify which faith a child will follow.

The agreement was oral. Like oral contracts for almost anything else, parties to an oral parenting agreement will often have different accounts of just what exactly the agreement was. As well, just like almost all other oral contacts, a court will not enforce an oral parenting agreement if the court cannot determine exactly what was agreed.

The agreement is very old. Many young couples that get married often wait a while before having children. If the couple made a parenting agreement a long time before they had their first child, or the agreement is old for any other reasons, a court may not lend that much weight to it.

Courts do not like to diminish First Amendment or parenting rights. Because of their importance, courts do not generally like to stomp down on the parenting or First Amendment rights of parents. In addition, courts do not generally like to issue orders that enforce prior-made parenting agreements as this can lead to excessive governmental involvement in the private lives of parents.

It is important to realize that not all courts dislike parenting agreements that discuss the religious upbringing of children. For example, in *Wilson v. Wilson*, an Indiana court ruled that a divorce agreement that contained terms regarding the religious education of the children was binding on the parents.

To sum up, if you think that you would like to have a parenting agreement that involves the religious education of your children, you should make sure that the agreement is very detailed, in writing and not more than a few years old.

General Advice

If you've learned anything from this article, it should be that the outcome of your case will depend greatly on the state that you are in. In addition, you should also realize that because there is no uniform national law that deals with this situation, the laws of your state could change at any time. Because of this, it is almost always better for you and the other parent to try to resolve any issues regarding child custody and religion outside of court.

If you fear that your child may be harmed, or is already being harmed by the religious activities of the other parent, you should try to take your child to a mental health professional. By bringing in experts, you may quiet your own fears by finding out that there are no risks of harm, or if there is harm, you will have evidence to support your case should you decide to go to court.

If you do end up going to court to resolve a situation involving child custody and religion, you should keep in mind that you have the best chance of success if you have sole or joint legal custody.

VIEWPOINT 5

> *"The court erred in failing to allow [the teenager] to live with the parent of his choice."*

An Older Teen May Have the Right to Decide Which Parent Has Custody

The South Carolina Supreme Court's Decision

James Brailsford

In the 1970 case Guinan v. Guinan, *Robert Guinan appealed a court decision that awarded his wife, Betty Guinan, custody of her children (whom he adopted). In the following viewpoint, a South Carolina Supreme Court justice argues that the previous court decision failed to consider the wishes of Guinan's son to live with his father. He suggests that the teen should have a choice, as evidence did not establish that living with his mother was in his best interests. James Brailsford served as an associate justice for the Supreme Court of South Carolina from 1962 to 1974.*

In this action for divorce, brought by the wife in the Richland County Court, the husband appeals from an adverse decree

James Brailsford, Opinion, *Guinan v. Guinan*, Supreme Court of South Carolina, July 28, 1970.

whereby the wife was awarded a divorce on the ground of physical cruelty and custody of a minor son and daughter, and the husband was ordered to convey to the wife his interest in the family residence, which inferentially, is owned by the parties as tenants in common, and all of the furniture therein.

The parties were married in 1961 and have no natural children of their own. The son and daughter are the children of the wife by a former marriage, and are the adopted children of the husband.

The first exception challenges the sufficiency of the evidence to establish physical cruelty within the meaning of the divorce statute. This exception must be sustained. In this respect, the complaint alleges only that on March 23, 1969, "the Defendant beat, hit, slapped and otherwise abused the Plaintiff, * * *." The scant record on appeal contains brief excerpts from the testimony of three witnesses, including the wife. This testimony is

Choosing one parent over another can be a difficult decision for teens. In many cases, courts take a teen's preference into serious consideration when awarding custody. © PhotoAlto/AP Images.

strictly confined to the one incident referred to in the complaint. It reveals nothing of the prior or subsequent relationship of the parties. The strongest inference which can be drawn from the testimony is that on this occasion, while quarreling, the husband and wife mutually engaged in a scuffle (shoving, pushing and pulling each other between two bedrooms) during which the husband choked the wife to some extent, sufficient to cause bruises on her throat. The wife did not testify that she was in fear of her husband either before, during or after this scuffle or that he applied sufficient pressure to her throat to cause her pain or to interfere with her breathing. The evidence is simply not susceptible of the inference that the husband's conduct on this occasion was of such atrocity as to take the case out of the general rule that a single act of physical cruelty does not constitute grounds for divorce, nor was there any evidence of precedent or attendant circumstances raising an apprehension that such act would likely be repeated. Hence, the evidence was insufficient to establish physical cruelty within the meaning of the statute.

Disregarding the Wishes of the Child

Without any findings of fact, other than her suitability as a custodian, the court awarded custody of the two children to the wife. At the time of the hearing the boy was sixteen years of age and in the eleventh grade in school. (He became seventeen on March 8, 1970, and, inferentially, is a rising high school senior.) As a witness, the boy stated that he regarded his adopted father as his real father and loved him as such, and that he preferred to live with him than to live with his mother. The father charges that the court erred in disregarding the wishes of the boy and awarding custody to the mother. We agree.

Ordinarily, the wishes of a child of this boy's age, intelligence and experience, although probably not controlling, are entitled to great weight in awarding his custody as between estranged parents. The court made no finding of fact tending to offset this important factor in awarding custody, and the record before us is

CHILDREN LIVING WITH ONLY ONE PARENT

More than one out of four children (26.2%) under 21 years old live with only one parent.

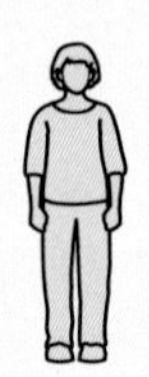

Taken From: US Census Bureau, "Custodial Mothers and Fathers and Their Child Support: 2009," December 2011.

bare of any evidence tending to do so. Absent any evidence tending to establish that the best interest of the boy would be served by awarding his custody to the mother, the court erred in failing to allow him to live with the parent of his choice.

We need not consider the grounds on which the husband challenges the order that he convey property to the wife. This provision of the decree was incidental to the award of a divorce to the wife and falls with the reversal of the divorce decree. The award of custody of the daughter to the mother is not involved on the appeal and is unaffected by our judgment. In other respects, the decree is Reversed.

VIEWPOINT 6

> *"The stability and companionship to be gained from keeping . . . children together is an important factor for the court to consider."*

Living Together After Divorce Is in the Best Interests of Siblings

The State of New York Court of Appeals' Decision

Matthew J. Jasen

In the 1982 case Eschbach v. Eschbach, *the New York Court of Appeals reversed a custody decision separating three sisters. For the two teenage sisters, the court awarded custody to their father, Donald Eschbach. The youngest sister, ten-year-old Laura, did not prefer either parent and was also to live with their father. However, another court modified the change in custody, and she remained with her mother. In the following viewpoint, a New York Court of Appeals justice maintains that it is in the best interest of the siblings to live together, requiring Laura to be under her father's custody. While their mother was not deemed an unfit parent, the author insists that Laura's strong desire to be with her sisters must be*

Matthew J. Jasen, Opinion, *Eschbach v. Eschbach*, Court of Appeals of the State of New York, May 13, 1982.

weighed, as siblings' companionship and stability promote welfare and happiness. Matthew J. Jasen retired from the New York Court of Appeals in 1985.

The question to be resolved on this appeal is whether custody of the youngest child of the parties herein should be changed, along with that of her two older sisters, from her mother to her father.

Plaintiff, Donald Eschbach, and defendant, Rita Eschbach, were married on November 23, 1963. Donald Eschbach was granted a divorce on May 28, 1979 on the basis of the couple having lived separate and apart pursuant to a separation agreement for one year. Custody of the three daughters of the marriage was granted to their mother pursuant to an oral stipulation of the parties entered in the minutes of the court at the inquest hearing held on January 16, 1979. The stipulation, which also provided visitation rights for the children's father, was incorporated but not merged in the judgment of divorce.

Events over the course of the next year indicated a progressive deterioration in the mother's relationship with her daughters. On several occasions, the two older girls, Karen and Ellen, ran away from [the] defendant's home, either to their father's residence or to friends' homes. The record also reveals that the mother refused to allow the girls to participate in extracurricular activities at school and imposed severe limitations on what activities they could participate in and with whom they were allowed to associate. Concerned that the children were being raised in an unhealthy atmosphere which was affecting their emotional and psychological development, the father commenced this action seeking a modification of the judgment of divorce to the extent of awarding him custody of his three daughters.

The Decision of the Trial Court

The trial court took testimony from both parents, representatives of the school, and the two older daughters. Although the youngest daughter, Laura, did not testify, she was interviewed by the court *in camera* [in a chamber], and a transcript of that proceeding is included in the record before us. Additionally, a report was prepared for the court by a probation officer who had interviewed the parties.

The trial court found that the mother's unreasonable demands and restrictions were jeopardizing the older daughters' emotional and intellectual development and that there was a total breakdown of communication between the older children and their mother. Furthermore, the court found that the strong preference to live with their father expressed by these children, who were age 16 and 14 at the time of the hearing, should be given consideration.

Although Laura, who was 10 at the time of the hearing, had not expressed a similarly strong preference to live with her father rather than her mother, the court recognized her strong desire to remain with her sisters. After considering all the factors presented, the court found that her best interests would be served by continuing her close relationship with her sisters and that a change of custody to her father was necessary under these circumstances.

On appeal, the Appellate Division agreed that "the antagonism [of the older] children * * * toward defendant and their strong preference to live with plaintiff" required a change in custody for Karen and Ellen. That court, however, modified the judgment and ordered that Laura's custody remain with the mother because there was "nothing to suggest that defendant has been anything but a fit parent toward her."

On this appeal, the father seeks custody of Laura. The mother has not sought a further appeal from that part of the order which affirmed the judgment awarding custody of Karen and Ellen to the plaintiff. The question on this appeal is thus limited to which parent should have custody of Laura. We agree with the trial court that Laura's best interests require a change in her custody from her mother to her father.

Determining the Child's Best Interests

Any court in considering questions of child custody must make every effort to determine "what is for the best interest of the child, and what will best promote its welfare and happiness." As we have recently stated, there are no absolutes in making these determinations; rather, there are policies designed not to bind the courts, but to guide them in determining what is in the best interests of the child.

Where the parties have entered into an agreement as to which parent should have custody, we have stated that "[p]riority, not as an absolute but as a weighty factor, should, in the absence of extraordinary circumstances, be accorded" to that agreement. This priority is afforded the first determination of custody in the belief the stability this policy will assure in the child's life is in the child's best interests. But as this court noted in *Friederwitzer* [*v. Friederwitzer*, 1982], "[n]o agreement of the parties can bind the court to a disposition other than that which a weighing of all the

Many courts have ruled in favor of keeping siblings together in the event of a divorce, arguing that it is in the children's best interest to grow up living together. © LWA/Getty Images.

factors involved shows to be in the child's best interests." Thus, an agreement between the parties is but one factor to be weighed by the court in deciding whether a change of custody is warranted.

The weight to be given the existence of a prior agreement depends on whether the prior disposition resulted from a full hearing by a trial court or was merely incorporated in the court's judgment pursuant to an uncontested stipulation. This is particularly true where, as in this case, the rules of the court require that the decree specify that "as to support, custody and visitation, no such agreement or stipulation is binding" and that the court retains jurisdiction for the purpose of making such further custody decree "as it finds appropriate under the circumstances existing at the time application for that purpose is made to it." Since the court was not bound by the existence of the prior agreement, it has the discretion to order custody changed "when the totality of circumstances, including the existence of the prior award, warrants its doing so in the best interests of the child."

Primary among those circumstances to be considered is the quality of the home environment and the parental guidance the custodial parent provides for the child. While concerns such as the financial status and the ability of each parent to provide for the child should not be overlooked by the court, an equally valid concern is the ability of each parent to provide for the child's emotional and intellectual development.

Cognizance of the Individual Needs of Each Child

In determining whether the custodial parent can continue to provide for the child's various needs, the court must be cognizant of the individual needs of each child. It is, of course, entirely possible that a circumstance such as a total breakdown in communication between a parent and child that would require a change in custody would be applicable only as to the best interests of one of several children. To this end, it is important for the court to consider the desires of each child. But again, this is but one factor to be considered; as with the other factors, the child's desires should not be considered determinative. While not determinative, the child's expressed preference is some indication of what is in the child's best interests. Of course, in weighing this factor, the court must consider the age and maturity of the child and the potential for influence having been exerted on the child.

Finally, this court has long recognized that it is often in the child's best interests to continue to live with his siblings. While this, too, is not an absolute, the stability and companionship to be gained from keeping the children together is an important factor for the court to consider. "Close familial relationships are much to be encouraged." "Young brothers and sisters need each other's strengths and association in their everyday and often common experiences, and to separate them, unnecessarily, is likely to be traumatic and harmful."

An Evaluation of All Parties Involved

The weighing of these various factors requires an evaluation of the testimony, character and sincerity of all the parties involved in this type of dispute. Generally, such an evaluation can best be made by the trial court which has direct access to the parties and can supplement that information with whatever professionally prepared reports are necessary. "In matters of this character 'the findings of the nisi prius court must be accorded the greatest respect'." Appellate courts should be reluctant to substitute their own evaluation of these subjective factors for that of the nisi prius court [the original trial court], and if they do, should articulate the reasons for so doing. Similarly, the existence or absence of any one factor cannot be determinative on appellate review since the court is to consider the totality of the circumstances.

Turning then to the facts of this case, we hold that the determination of the trial court that the totality of the circumstances warrants awarding custody of Laura to her father conforms to the weight of the evidence. The record indicates that although the mother is not an unfit parent for Laura, she is, under all the

Easing the Transition

Many children in divorced families provide each other with support and continuity that help to ease the transition. Mara, who was seven, and Jennifer, who was four when their adoptive parents divorced, recalled in an interview with me how important it was for them to have each other when everything in their lives seemed to change. Jennifer spoke of how Mara's presence made her feel safer when she visited her father in his new apartment. She could count on Jennifer to braid her hair and to encourage her father to buy the foods she liked. Things did not seem so different with Mara there to help her.

When their parents eventually remarried, Mara and Jennifer found it easier to deal with their stepparents because they had each other. If they thought they were not being treated fairly they had each other to complain to. The support these sisters offered each other during their parents' divorce and remarriage led to an extremely close bond between them that continued through their adulthood.

Joyce Edward, The Sibling Relationship: A Force for Growth and Conflict. *Lanham, MD: Jason Aronson, 2011.*

circumstances present here, the less fit parent. Thus, the trial court was not bound by the stipulation of the parties, but was free to, and indeed required to, review the totality of the circumstances to determine what would be in Laura's best interests. In doing so, the Trial Judge weighed the testimony of all the parties, including Laura, and considered the testimony of school officials and reports from a probation officer appointed by the court. The court made no specific finding that [the] defendant was an unfit mother for Laura, but a finding that the mother was the less fit parent is implicit in its order to change custody and is supported by the record. Additionally, the trial court, while noting Laura's ambivalence as to which parent she would prefer to live with, gave significant weight to her strong desire to remain with her older sisters. The record indicates that all relevant factors, including the mother's ability to cope with raising children as they approach maturity and the father's desire to provide a fuller and more enriched environment for his daughters were considered. It is abundantly clear from the record that the trial court, in this case, made a careful and studied review of all the relevant factors. As the determination of the nisi prius court, we believe this holding should be accorded great deference on review.

Accordingly, the order of the Appellate Division should be reversed, without costs, and the judgment of Supreme Court, Westchester County, reinstated.

Order reversed, etc.

Viewpoint

> *"A sibling does not have standing to seek court ordered visitation with a minor sibling where not specifically authorized to do so by statute."*

Siblings May Not Have Visitation Rights

The Pennsylvania Supreme Court's Decision

John P. Flaherty Jr.

In C.R. v. Arthur Z. and Mary Jane Z. *(1996), Ken R., on behalf of his daughter, C.R., filed suit for visitation rights with her half-sisters. In the following viewpoint, a Pennsylvania Supreme Court justice states that siblings cannot seek court-ordered visitation with a minor sibling if it is not authorized by statute. He recognizes the importance of siblings to maintain contact, but persists that Pennsylvania law does not protect C.R.'s interest, and such rights are not judicially extended to her. John P. Flaherty Jr. served as a justice in the Supreme Court of Pennsylvania from 1978 to 2001.*

Appellant, Ken R., on behalf of his daughter, C.R., appeals from the order of the Superior Court affirming the order of the Court of Common Pleas of Lehigh County which found that

John P. Flaherty Jr., Opinion, *C.R. v. Arthur Z. and Mary Jane Z.*, Supreme Court of Pennsylvania, October 4, 1996.

Appellant did not have standing to sue for visitation privileges with her half-sisters. For the reasons that follow, we affirm.

C.R. is the daughter of Ken R. and Mary Jane Z. In 1981, Ken R. and Mary Jane Z. divorced, and Mary Jane Z. took custody of C.R. Subsequently, Mary Jane Z. married Arthur Z., and they had two daughters.

C.R. continued to live with Mary Jane Z., Arthur Z, and their two daughters until 1993. At that time, C.R. accused Arthur Z. of sexual molestation. Although Arthur Z. denied the accusation, the parties agreed upon a Protection from Abuse Order, and C.R. went to live with her father, Ken R.

Mary Jane Z. did not believe C.R.'s accusation, and the incident caused a great deal of discord in their relationship. As a result of the incident, Mary Jane Z. has refused to allow C.R. to see her two half-sisters.

In 1993, Ken R. filed suit on behalf of his daughter C.R. seeking visitation rights with her half-sisters. Mary Jane and Arthur Z. filed an Answer and New Matter which asserted, among other things, that C.R. did not have standing to bring such a visitation action.

The trial court agreed with Mary Jane and Arthur Z. and dismissed the complaint for visitation. In so doing, it held that because siblings are not included in the statutory language governing custody and visitation, such rights could not be judicially extended to them. The trial court relied on *Weber v. Weber* [1988] . . . for the proposition that because of the fundamental right to rear one's children free from governmental intrusion, standing to interfere with a parent's right to custody is limited only to those individuals specifically allowed by statute.

No Legal Right to Interfere in the Absence of Statutory Authority

The Superior Court affirmed. . . . It found that it was constrained to agree with the trial court and was bound by the decision in *Weber v. Weber*. . . . The Superior Court's decision was based on the conclusion that the legislature has not given siblings the statutory authority to interfere with the parents' decision not to allow sibling visitation and that there is no legal right to interfere in the absence of statutory authority. Thus, the Superior Court held that a sibling lacks standing to maintain a partial custody or visitation action against both parents of a minor sibling.

This appeal followed, and we granted allocatur [allowance of a proceeding] to determine whether a sibling has standing to seek court ordered visitation with a minor sibling, although not specifically authorized to do so by statute. For the reasons that follow, we are constrained to hold that a sibling does not have standing to seek court ordered visitation with a minor sibling.

Both the trial court and the Superior Court relied on *Weber v. Weber* . . . wherein the Superior Court held that an adult sibling did not have standing to seek partial custody of her minor sister. In *Weber*, the adult sibling was unmarried and lived with an unmarried man in a residence separate from her parents and minor sister. Mrs. Weber did not approve of this living arrangement and, therefore, did not allow the minor sister to visit with her adult sister. Based on the parents' right to raise their children as they see fit and the lack of statutory authority for a sibling to request court intervention, the court in *Weber* found that the sibling relationship failed to give rise to a legal right to seek partial custody.

C.R. submits that this Court should not follow the analysis in *Weber, supra;* rather, this Court should adopt the reasoning of the Superior Court of New Jersey in *L. v. G.* [1985] . . . wherein that court held that adult siblings have standing to seek visitation with their minor siblings, despite the fact that the New Jersey legislature had only afforded the privilege of visiting with minor children to grandparents. The court in *L. v. G.*, stated that "the right to visit with one's own brother or sister is equal to, if not greater than the right to visit with one's grandchildren." Thus, the New Jersey Superior Court found that siblings, when in the child's best interests, possess the inherent right to visit each other. However, in light of our case law and the principles of statutory construction, we are constrained to find that siblings do not have standing to seek court ordered visitation with their siblings in Pennsylvania.

Qualifying for Court-Ordered Visitation Rights

In order to have standing, a "party must (a) have a substantial interest in the subject-matter of the litigation; (b) the interest must be direct; and (c) the interest must be immediate and not a remote consequence." [As stated in *S. Whitehall TP v. South Whitehall*, 1989]:

> A "substantial" interest is an interest in the outcome of the litigation which surpasses the common interest of all citizens in procuring obedience to the law. A "direct" interest requires a showing that the matter complained of caused harm to the party's interest. An "immediate" interest involves the nature of the causal connection between the action complained of and the injury to the party challenging it and is shown where the interest the party seeks to protect is within the zone of interests sought to be protected by the statute or constitutional guarantee in question.

In this case, C.R. has a substantial interest in maintaining her relationship with her sisters. Clearly, as a sibling, C.R.'s interests in this matter far outweigh any interest of the citizenry in general. C.R. also has a direct interest. C.R. cannot maintain her relationship with her two half-sisters because of the actions of Mary Jane Z. Presently, her only means of maintaining a relationship with her two half-sisters is through the court system because Mary Jane Z. has forbidden all contact between C.R. and her two half-sisters. However, C.R. does not have an immediate interest and, therefore, does not have standing to seek court ordered visitation with her two half-siblings.

As stated above, an immediate interest is shown where the interest the party seeks to protect is within the zone of interests sought to be protected by the statute or constitutional guarantee in question. The General Assembly has declared the zone of interests it seeks to protect as follows:

> [I]t is the public policy of this Commonwealth, when in the best interest of the child, *to assure a reasonable and continuing contact of the child with both parents* after a separation or dissolution of the marriage and the sharing of the rights and responsibilities of child rearing by both parents *and continuing contact of the child or children with grandparents when a parent is deceased, divorced or separated.*

Applying the rules of statutory construction, the inclusion of a specific matter in a statute implies the exclusion of other matters. There is no provision in the statute for protecting C.R.'s interest, that is maintaining her relationship with her sisters. Thus, C.R.'s interest does not fall within the zone of interests that the statute seeks to protect.

The statute recognizes the right of parents to raise their children as they see fit without unwarranted governmental intrusion. This right has been recognized as one of our basic and fundamental rights. With this in mind, the legislature has allowed court interference with the parents' right to custody only in rare and exceptional circumstances. . . .

The Importance of Sibling Relationships

C.R. argues that if courts can order children in custody cases to see a counselor, a psychologist, a reading tutor, or even a friend, they must be able to order siblings to see each other. She submits that if the courts are powerless to order sibling visitation, then there is a gaping hole in our child custody jurisprudence.

First, we must note that a judge can only order a child to see someone after it has been determined that the petitioning party has standing to seek the relief requested. Additionally, we are well aware that the application of the law of standing in this case

An adult sibling is not always granted visitation rights to a minor sibling even if such interactions could be beneficial to the child. © GSO Images/Getty Images.

may lead to an unfortunate result. However, we must be mindful that the legislature has made an explicit pronouncement on the subject of custody and visitation. Clearly, the legislature expressed a concern, when in the best interests of the child, for continuing contact of a child with both parents and, in certain circumstances, a child with grandparents. There is nothing in the

Sibling Visitation Is Rarely an Issue

When siblings are placed in different households, courts typically arrange visitation time between each child and the parent who is not the custodial parent of the child so that the visiting child also spends time with his or her siblings. Thus, there is rarely an issue of sibling visitation postdivorce. If a court failed to do so, however, and the parents did not independently arrange for siblings to spend time together, the question would arise whether children have a right to maintain contact with each other, a right that limits the decision-making authority states confer on parents as a component of custody.

James G. Dwyer, The Relationship Rights of Children. *New York: Cambridge University Press, 2006.*

statute, however, that protects the interests of siblings to sue for visitation.

This does not lessen the well established importance this Court has placed on sibling relationships. In this case, the Superior Court echoed the concerns raised by Judge [John G.] Brosky in his concurring opinion in *Weber:*

> The relationships between siblings should be closely guarded and nurtured, since it is those relationships that will provide a harbor from which a child may find [his or] her way through the often turbulent waters of life. While it is true that parents may serve this function as well, we must realize that more often than not, parents predecease their children, creating the situation where siblings must comfort, support and depend upon each other. Even in less drastic circumstances, because siblings are closer in age and have shared life experiences, it would be quite natural for them to seek each other's counsel and companionship on routine matters as well.

We wholeheartedly agree with the sentiments expressed in the above passage. However, these concerns do not rise to the level of a legal interest where the legislature has enacted a specific statute addressing custody and visitation and has not included rights of children to seek court ordered visitation with siblings.

Therefore, we are constrained to hold that a sibling does not have standing to seek court ordered visitation with a minor sibling where not specifically authorized to do so by statute. We take this opportunity, as did the trial court and Superior Court in this case, to recommend that the legislature reexamine this area of the law and consider whether siblings should have a legal interest to sue for visitation.

Accordingly, we affirm the order of the Superior Court.

VIEWPOINT

"Visitation conceived as a parental right marginalizes both the children's relational interests and the nurture and care of children."

Visitation Decisions Must Include Non-traditional Relationships

Ayelet Blecher-Prigat

In the following viewpoint, a university lecturer asserts that visitation understood solely as a parental right does not serve the best interests of children. According to the author, children form meaningful attachments beyond their parents—grandparents, stepparents, and other adult relatives—that are essential to their social development. The current legal approach nonetheless views nonparent visitation as intrusive on the custodian-child relationship, she contends, and treats children as the property of parents. Ayelet Blecher-Prigat is a guest lecturer at the Faculty of Law at Bar-Ilan University in Israel.

The primary consideration in awarding visitation, from the children's perspective, is to maintain the continuity of meaningful relationships in their lives. Further, when adults are

Ayelet Blecher-Prigat, "Rethinking Visitation: From a Parental to a Relational Right," *Duke Journal of Gender Law & Policy*, vol. 16, no. 1, 2009, pp. 15–19, 26–28.

concerned, awarding visitation should primarily reward nurture and care for children rather than the biological relationship of the adult to the child. Visitation conceived as a parental right marginalizes both the children's relational interests and the nurture and care of children. It instead emphasizes considerations such as biology that, while not entirely irrelevant, should be secondary in constructing a right to visitation. The emphasis on biology and parental status leaves room for remnants of the perception of children as their parents' property and policy considerations that elevate marriage and the nuclear family as superior institutions.

Questioning the prevalent understanding of visitation as a parental right does not suggest that parents are not normally entitled to visitation or do not have a special relationship with their children that is qualitatively different from the relationships children have with grandparents, stepparents, and other relatives. By the theory presented in this [viewpoint], most parents would still be entitled to visitation rights. The basis for this entitlement, however, would be their active role as parents in nurturing and caring for their children rather than their parental status.

Children's Relational Interests

In light of the central role that children's interests should play in constructing the legal rules that affect them, this section begins the case against the conception of visitation as a parental right by discussing children's interests in the issue of visitation. Talking about children's interests in order to challenge (and even more so in order to justify) adults' rights requires a short pause. Children's interests can and often should be protected through children's own rights. Recognizing children's rights, however, does not preclude recognizing adults' rights in relation to children. If we cherish children's interests, however, we should guarantee that when there are available two alternative legal models for recognizing adults' interests and protecting them through rights, the preferable one is the one more compatible with children's interests.

The current consensus on children's relational interests is that children can form multiple relationships, which are essential for their social developmental needs. Time with legal parents is insufficient to meet those needs, and grandparents, other adult relatives, stepparents, and other adults play roles in children's lives. When all the relationships a child enjoys are consensual, a child will only benefit from this broad web of multiple relationships. Dilemmas arise when one of the child's existing or potential relationships is not welcomed by the child's custodial parent, creating a situation that will lead to a demand for visitation rights.

Two less than ideal alternatives exist in these cases. The first is to maintain the multiple relationships in the child's life while exposing her to conflict and burdening her relationship with her custodian. The second is to preserve a stable relationship with the custodian parent and allow additional relationships only as approved by the child's custodian.

The Extreme of Eliminating Non-Custodial Visitation

Preference for stability in a child's life based on protecting her relationship with her custodian is the position that [child psychiatry and law experts] Joseph Goldstein, Anna Freud, and Albert Solnit adopt. Their stance is also the most extreme, since they suggest that, following divorce, even visitation rights of non-custodial parents should be eliminated. They do not disregard the significance of the relationship between children and their non-custodial parents. Indeed, their advice in situations of divorce is to encourage custodial parents to facilitate visitation between the non-custodial parent and the child. They even suggest that, other things being equal, courts should award custody to the parent most willing to provide the child opportunities for contact with the other parent. They argue, however, that children benefit from multiple ties on the condition that the relationships between the adults involved are positive, or at least not hostile and negative.

Children often thrive in family relationships that stretch beyond their biological parents and that include multiple generations. © Jack Hollingsworth/Getty Images.

In their view, any visitation the custodial parent considers undesirable may expose the child to conflicting loyalties, compromise the intimacy between the child and the custodial parent, and shatter the child's required trust in the parent's autonomy when exercising control over the child's life. Goldstein, Freud, and Solnit further contend that the threat that compulsory visitation poses to the child's relationship with her custodian is in no way offset by any of visitation's potential benefits, due to the limited relationship a child can form with an individual who is merely visiting. They also argue that facilitating children's positive relationships with two people in conflict with one another is beyond the courts' capacity.

Goldstein, Freud, and Solnit's position is rather extreme, as noted, and highly controversial in academic circles. Their numerous critics focus on the benefits of maintaining multiple relationships in children's lives, despite potential conflicts. Studies conducted in various contexts point out the significance of continued relationships in children's lives, and the harmful effects to the child of losing a significant relationship. Studies of families after divorce show that maintaining ties with non-custodial parents through visitation is highly significant for children. Data on foster placement and on the adoption of older children also indicate that continued contact with the original parents generally promotes the child's sense of well-being and emotional security. Cross-cultural research has expanded the framework of discussion, pointing out that children form multiple attachments not only to parents but also to psychological parents and to others who are members of their kin groups. In various cultures, raising and caring for children is not the sole responsibility of parents; grandparents and other relatives assume care giving roles and thus play a significant role in a child's life. In these various contexts of analysis—divorce, foster care, adoption, and cultural scenarios—advocates of expanding the web of relationships in children's lives point to the potential harm entailed by the loss of a meaningful relationship. They argue that it exceeds the harm of a conflicting relationship and the potential harm to the relationship between the child and her custodian.

For the purpose of this [viewpoint], we do not need to take sides in this dilemma. The relevant data are confused and unreliable, and probably no single answer can contend with all cases. Advocates of maintaining multiple relationships in children's lives, *inter alia* [among other things] by awarding rights of visitation, focus on the continuity of meaningful relationships in children's lives rather than on establishing new ones. From the perspective of children's interests, then, visitation laws should rely primarily on the existence or absence of a relationship with the child.

The Inconsistency of the Legal Approach

In the prevalent perception of visitation as a parental right, non-parents are generally denied visitation rights, even when visitation is meant to preserve an ongoing relationship with a child. By contrast, "parents," once legally defined as such, are entitled to visitations even without any previous relationship with the child. This legal distinction seems incompatible with the interest in maintaining the continuity of meaningful relationships in children's lives.

Furthermore, when visitation laws rely on parental status, results are inconsistent and incoherent. In some contexts the law supports multiple relationships, even if they are conflicting. In other contexts the law supports safeguarding one unconditional attachment for the child, even at the expense of severing other relationships. When the claimant for visitation is a non-parent, the law prefers to maintain one unconditional relationship with the child, and views legally enforced visitation as an intrusion on the custodian-child relationship. The law rejects this perception of visitation rights, however, when the claimant is a legally recognized parent. Sustaining multiple, even conflicting, attachments in children's lives is viewed as the best, not just the least detrimental, alternative when the child's parents are involved.

The inconsistency, however, could be merely apparent. A distinction between parents and non-parents seems entirely justified, since parents play the most significant role in children's lives. But parents are so significant because most parents raise and nurture their children, not because of their parental status. And yet . . . parental status cannot serve as a sufficiently adequate proxy for significant relationships in children's lives that should be preserved through rights of visitation. . . .

The Concept of "Children as Property"

Parents are entitled to visitations even without any previous relationship with the child, as noted, and the parental status-based legal distinction. This implies that visitation rules do not seek to protect children's meaningful attachments and that those rules rest instead on other considerations. . . . Incorporating and protecting adults' interests in relation to children generally and parents' interests specifically is not inherently objectionable. In

The Third-Party Visitation Movement

Until the mid-1960s, it was almost impossible for someone other than a legally recognized parent to sue a parent for the right to custody or visitation of the parent's child. Then the law gradually began to change. New York was among the first states to enact a third-party visitation statute. Its statute, which in hindsight may seem modest, was almost revolutionary. It authorized grandparents to seek court-ordered visitation of their grandchildren over a parent's objection when one of the parents died or when the parents divorced. Before the remarkable lobbying effort of the American Association of Retired Persons was finished, every state in the country (the District of Columbia is the only exception) enacted a statute authorizing grandparents to seek court-ordered visitation. Indeed, the idea became so attractive to many legislators that what began as a grandparent movement was rapidly expanded to other designated third parties (such as aunts, uncles, siblings, nonmarital partners, stepparents, and foster parents) and, in the most ambitious of states, to "any person."

Martin Guggenheim, What's Wrong With Children's Rights?. *Cambridge, MA: Harvard University Press, 2005.*

the visitation context, however, the recognition and protection of parents' private interests embodies the remnants of the notorious conception of children as their parents' property, which should be eliminated from current jurisprudence.

The disturbing history of children construed as chattels and as their parents' property is well known. This perception has been abandoned at the declaratory level and all—courts, legislators, and legal scholars—today vehemently reject any such characterization. But although we would like to think that the conception of children as property belongs only in legal history textbooks, many child advocates have shown that it still casts a shadow. [Child rights expert] Barbara Bennett Woodhouse, for example, demonstrated how doctrines of parental rights, developed at a time when children were still treated as quasi-property, embody and continue to perpetuate this conception.

When treated as a parental right, visitation laws show traces of this view, which is manifest, above all, in the language of entitlement. That language accompanies parental visitation rights, regardless of whether the parents have an established relationship with the child. The proprietary roots of this parental entitlement are further evident in the quid pro quo approach that accompanies parents' rights in general and parental visitation rights in particular. The common reasoning whereby the payment of child support entitles the father to a certain amount of visitation is an expression of this approach.

The strength of parents' visitation rights and the reluctance to deny them, even if the parents are abusive, as well as the traditional exclusivity of parental rights regarding visitation, further attest to the parents' proprietary interests in their children. Exclusive possession and right of use characterize traditional conceptions of private property. According to this exclusivity rule, then, children are depicted as property and access to them is a private good to which only the owner-parents should be entitled. The proprietary roots of visitation rights as parental rights can also account, at least partly, for the fact that grandparents have been much more successful than other non-parents in ensuring recognition to their claims for visitation. Special provisions included in many state statutes ensure the grandparents' visitation rights upon the death of their child, their grandchild's parent. Grandparents thus inherit from their child right of access to their grandchild.

> *"The extension of statutory rights in [visitation] to persons other than a child's parents, however, comes with an obvious cost."*

Parents Have the Right to Limit Visitation of Grandparents

The US Supreme Court's Decision

Sandra Day O'Connor

In Troxel v. Granville *(2000), the US Supreme Court ruled against the child visitation rights of grandparents, overriding a Washington state statute allowing third parties to seek visitation. The Troxels, paternal grandparents to the children of Tommie Granville, filed suit after Granville limited their visits. In the following viewpoint, a Supreme Court justice maintains that third parties have no child visitation rights. She claims that it interferes with the constitutional right of parents to raise their children. Furthermore, she points out that the statute—under which a state court ruled in the Troxels' favor—is overly broad and can overturn any fit parent's decision regarding child visitation. Sandra Day O'Connor was the first woman to be elected to the Supreme Court and served as an associate justice from 1981 to 2006.*

Sandra Day O'Connor, Opinion, *Troxel v. Granville*, US Supreme Court, June 5, 2000.

The demographic changes of the past century make it difficult to speak of an average American family. The composition of families varies greatly from household to household. While many children may have two married parents and grandparents who visit regularly, many other children are raised in single-parent households. In 1996, children living with only one parent accounted for 28 percent of all children under age 18 in the United States. Understandably, in these single-parent households, persons outside the nuclear family are called upon with increasing frequency to assist in the everyday tasks of child rearing. In many cases, grandparents play an important role. For example, in 1998, approximately 4 million children—or 5.6 percent of all children under age 18—lived in the household of their grandparents.

The nationwide enactment of nonparental visitation statutes is assuredly due, in some part, to the States' recognition of these changing realities of the American family. Because grandparents and other relatives undertake duties of a parental nature in many households, States have sought to ensure the welfare of the children therein by protecting the relationships those children form with such third parties. The States' nonparental visitation statutes are further supported by a recognition, which varies from State to State, that children should have the opportunity to benefit from relationships with statutorily specified persons—for example, their grandparents. The extension of statutory rights in this area to persons other than a child's parents, however, comes with an obvious cost. For example, the State's recognition of an independent third-party interest in a child can place a substantial burden on the traditional parent-child relationship. Contrary to [Supreme Court Justice John Paul] Stevens' accusation, our description of state nonparental visitation statutes in these terms, of course, is not meant to suggest that "children are so much chattel." Rather, our terminology is intended to highlight the fact that these statutes can present questions of constitutional import. In this case, we are presented with just such a question. Specifically, we are asked to decide whether § 26.10.160(3), as applied to Tommie Granville and her family, violates the Federal Constitution.

The Fourteenth Amendment and the Fundamental Right of Parents

The Fourteenth Amendment provides that no State shall "deprive any person of life, liberty, or property, without due process of law." We have long recognized that the Amendment's Due Process Clause, like its Fifth Amendment counterpart, "guarantees more than fair process." *Washington v. Glucksberg* [1997]. . . . The Clause also includes a substantive component that "provides heightened protection against government interference with certain fundamental rights and liberty interests."

US Supreme Court Justice Sandra Day O'Connor, seen here in 2006, wrote the Court opinion stating that third parties, including grandparents, do not have rights to child visitation. © AP Images.

The liberty interest at issue in this case—the interest of parents in the care, custody, and control of their children—is perhaps the oldest of the fundamental liberty interests recognized by this Court. More than 75 years ago [in 2000], in *Meyer v. Nebraska* [1923] . . . we held that the "liberty" protected by the Due Process Clause includes the right of parents to "establish a home and bring up children" and "to control the education of their own." Two years later, in *Pierce v. Society of Sisters* [1925] . . . we again held that the "liberty of parents and guardians" includes the right "to direct the upbringing and education of children under their control." We explained in *Pierce* that "[t]he child is not the mere creature of the State; those who nurture him and direct his destiny have the right, coupled with the high duty, to recognize and prepare him for additional obligations." We returned to the subject in *Prince v. Massachusetts* [1944] . . . and again confirmed that there is a constitutional dimension to the right of parents to direct the upbringing of their children:

> It is cardinal with us that the custody, care and nurture of the child reside first in the parents, whose primary function and freedom include preparation for obligations the state can neither supply nor hinder.

In subsequent cases also, we have recognized the fundamental right of parents to make decisions concerning the care, custody, and control of their children. . . .

In light of this extensive precedent, it cannot now be doubted that the Due Process Clause of the Fourteenth Amendment protects the fundamental right of parents to make decisions concerning the care, custody, and control of their children.

Disregarding and Overturning the Parent's Decision

Section 26.10.160(3), as applied to Granville and her family in this case, unconstitutionally infringes on that fundamental parental right. The Washington nonparental visitation statute is breathtakingly broad. According to the statute's text, "*[a]ny person* may petition the court for visitation rights *at any time*," and the court may grant such visitation rights whenever "visitation may serve *the best interest of the child*." That language effectively permits any third party seeking visitation to subject any decision by a parent concerning visitation of the parent's children to state-court review. Once the visitation petition has been filed in court and the matter is placed before a judge, a parent's decision that visitation would not be in the child's best interest is accorded no deference. Section 26.10.160(3) contains no requirement that a court accord the parent's decision any presumption of validity or any weight whatsoever. Instead, the Washington statute places the best-interest determination solely in the hands of the judge. Should the judge disagree with the parent's estimation of the child's best interests, the judge's view necessarily prevails. Thus, in practical effect, in the State of Washington a court can disregard and overturn *any* decision by a fit custodial parent concerning visitation whenever a third party affected by the decision files a visitation petition, based solely on the judge's determination of the child's best interests. The Washington Supreme Court had the opportunity to give § 26.10.160(3) a narrower reading, but it declined to do so.

Turning to the facts of this case, the record reveals that the Superior Court's order was based on precisely the type of mere disagreement we have just described and nothing more. The Superior Court's order was not founded on any special factors that might justify the State's interference with Granville's fundamental right to make decisions concerning the rearing of her two daughters. To be sure, this case involves a visitation petition filed by grandparents soon after the death of their son—the father of Isabelle and Natalie—but the combination of several factors here compels our conclusion that § 26.10.160(3), as applied, exceeded the bounds of the Due Process Clause.

First, the Troxels did not allege, and no court has found, that Granville was an unfit parent. That aspect of the case is important, for there is a presumption that fit parents act in the best interests of their children. As this Court explained in *Parham* [*v. J.R.*, 1979]:

> [O]ur constitutional system long ago rejected any notion that a child is the mere creature of the State and, on the contrary, asserted that parents generally have the right, coupled with the high duty, to recognize and prepare [their children] for additional obligations. . . . The law's concept of the family rests on a presumption that parents possess what a child lacks in maturity, experience, and capacity for judgment required for making life's difficult decisions. More important, historically it has recognized that natural bonds of affection lead parents to act in the best interests of their children.

Accordingly, so long as a parent adequately cares for his or her children (*i.e.*, is fit), there will normally be no reason for the State to inject itself into the private realm of the family to further question the ability of that parent to make the best decisions concerning the rearing of that parent's children.

Contravening a Fit Parent's Rights

The problem here is not that the Washington Superior Court intervened, but that when it did so, it gave no special weight at all to Granville's determination of her daughters' best interests. More importantly, it appears that the Superior Court applied exactly the opposite presumption. In reciting its oral ruling after the conclusion of closing arguments, the Superior Court judge explained:

> The burden is to show that it is in the best interest of the children to have some visitation and some quality time with their grandparents. I think in most situations a commonsensical approach [is that] it is normally in the best interest of the children to spend quality time with the grandparent, unless the grandparent, *[sic]* there are some issues or problems involved wherein the grandparents, their lifestyles are going to impact

adversely upon the children. That certainly isn't the case here from what I can tell.

The judge's comments suggest that he presumed the grandparents' request should be granted unless the children would be "impact[ed] adversely." In effect, the judge placed on Granville, the fit custodial parent, the burden of *disproving* that visitation would be in the best interest of her daughters. The judge reiterated moments later: "I think [visitation with the Troxels] would be in the best interest of the children and I haven't been shown it is not in [the] best interest of the children."

The decisional framework employed by the Superior Court directly contravened the traditional presumption that a fit parent will act in the best interest of his or her child. In that respect, the court's presumption failed to provide any protection for Granville's fundamental constitutional right to make decisions concerning the rearing of her own daughters.

In an ideal world, parents might always seek to cultivate the bonds between grandparents and their grandchildren. Needless to say, however, our world is far from perfect, and in it the decision whether such an intergenerational relationship would be beneficial in any specific case is for the parent to make in the first instance. And, if a fit parent's decision of the kind at issue here becomes subject to judicial review, the court must accord at least some special weight to the parent's own determination.

Finally, we note that there is no allegation that Granville ever sought to cut off visitation entirely. Rather, the present dispute originated when Granville informed the Troxels that she would prefer to restrict their visitation with Isabelle and Natalie to one short visit per month and special holidays. See 87 Wash. App., at 133, 940 P. 2d, at 699; Verbatim Report 12. In the Superior Court proceedings Granville did not oppose visitation but instead asked that the duration of any visitation order be shorter than that requested by the Troxels. While the Troxels requested two weekends per month and two full weeks in the summer,

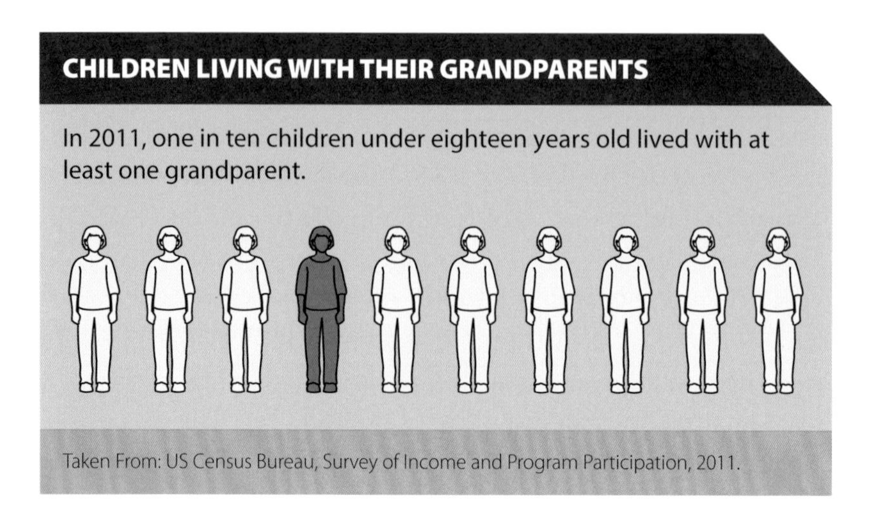

Granville asked the Superior Court to order only one day of visitation per month (with no overnight stay) and participation in the Granville family's holiday celebrations. The Superior Court gave no weight to Granville's having assented to visitation even before the filing of any visitation petition or subsequent court intervention. The court instead rejected Granville's proposal and settled on a middle ground, ordering one weekend of visitation per month, one week in the summer, and time on both of the petitioning grandparents' birthdays.

Judges Cannot Make "Better" Child-Rearing Decisions

Considered together with the Superior Court's reasons for awarding visitation to the Troxels, the combination of these factors demonstrates that the visitation order in this case was an unconstitutional infringement on Granville's fundamental right to make decisions concerning the care, custody, and control of her two daughters. The Washington Superior Court failed to accord the determination of Granville, a fit custodial parent, any material weight. In fact, the Superior Court made only two formal findings in support of its visitation order. First, the Troxels "are part of a large, central, loving family, all located in this area, and the [Troxels] can provide opportunities for the children in the areas of cousins and music." Second, "[t]he children would be benefitted from spending quality time with the [Troxels], provided that that time is balanced with time with the childrens' *[sic]* nuclear family." These slender findings, in combination with the court's announced presumption in favor of grandparent visitation and its failure to accord significant weight to Granville's already having offered meaningful visitation to the Troxels, show that this case involves nothing more than a simple disagreement between the Washington Superior Court and Granville concerning her children's best interests. The Superior Court's announced reason for ordering one week of visitation in the summer demonstrates our conclusion well: "I look back on some personal experiences. . . . We always spen[t] as kids a week with one set of grandparents and another set of grandparents, [and] it happened to work out in our family that [it] turned out to be an enjoyable experience. Maybe that can, in this family, if that is how it works out." As we have explained, the Due Process Clause does not permit a State to infringe on the fundamental right of parents to make child rearing decisions simply because a state judge believes a "better" decision could be made. Neither the Washington nonparental visitation statute generally—which places no limits on either the persons who may petition for visitation or the circumstances in which such a petition may be granted—nor the Superior Court in this specific case required anything more. Accordingly, we hold that § 26.10.160(3), as applied in this case, is unconstitutional.

VIEWPOINT 10

> *"Seeing Mom and Dad each day is sort of like the experience someone would have living with married parents and seeing them both all the time."*

How I Divide My Life Between My Divorced Parents' Homes

Personal Narrative

Juergens

In the following viewpoint, a teen describes how joint custody, in which she switches between her mother's and father's house every other day, has provided her with a stable home and close bonds with each parent. Dividing her time and life equally, she claims, creates an arrangement similar to having married parents and serves as a model for other divorced families. In addition, the author says that having their divorce take place when she was two years old lessened its negative impacts on her. At the time of publication, Juergens was a high school freshman in Brooklyn, New York.

Juergens, "Equal Time: How I Divide My Life Between My Divorced Parents' Homes," *Newsweek*, December 14, 2008. www.thedailybeast.com/newsweek.

My parents divorced when I was 2 years old. Because I was so young, I cannot remember anything of how the divorce actually felt at the time. But 12 years later, I am quite content with my life and my parents. Unlike many divorced couples with children, neither parent has primary custody of me, but rather, I switch between my parents' houses every other day, spending roughly equal time with my mother and my father.

When I describe the system to other kids, many of them gape at me and are absolutely baffled. "How I can stand my life being so crazy and confusing?" they ask. Others frankly say that my parents are weird for not doing some kind of every-other-weekend deal. I always respond by explaining how after all this time, the routine seems like normal and isn't confusing at all and that I would honestly not have it any other way.

I believe that I am a significantly more stable person because I get to see both my mom and dad so frequently. I don't think that my relationships with either of them would be as loving and open as they are, if I even switched houses every week, because for me at least, seeing both parents every day makes me closer with both of them. They both always know what's going on in my life, and there isn't that awkwardness of having to explain to one what happened during a week where they weren't part of my life. I have had a more "normal" experience growing up, in that seeing Mom and Dad each day is sort of like the experience someone would have living with married parents and seeing them both all the time.

It's definitely an essential component of my happiness as a person that my parents have found a way to be friends even though things didn't work out between them during their married life. After the divorce, no one would have blamed my parents if they never wanted to talk to each other again. But Mom and Dad rose above the anger they felt for each other, and focused on the 2-year-old daughter they had. They made what I believe is undoubtedly the right choice, by arranging it so that both of them would be able to see me daily and, when around me at least,

JOINT VERSUS PRIMARY CUSTODY AFTER DIVORCE

Percent of primary custody and joint custody arrangements in the United States.

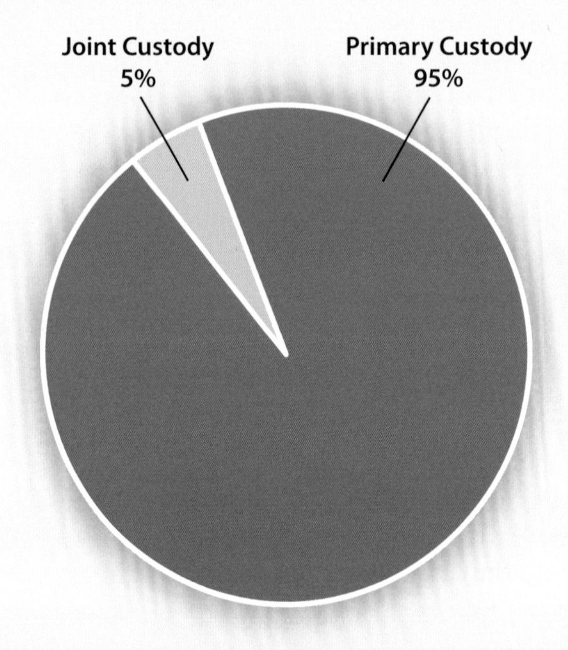

Taken From: Joan B. Kelly, "Children's Living Arrangements Following Separation and Divorce: Insights from Empirical and Clinical Research," *Family Process*, vol. 46, no. 1, 2007.

acting in a friendly manner toward each other. Eventually, after a while of being friendly, they actually became friends. Now I might even venture to say that they are among each other's best friends.

The way my parents have dealt with their divorce has been an inspiration to many other couples with children going through the same thing. Some of my friends' parents have used my family as a mentor to create similar arrangements between their kid and themselves.

Not only am I happy with the system my parents have, but I am also extremely grateful that Mom and Dad divorced in the first place. If they had stayed together, I am sure that there would be tons more fighting, unhappiness and disrespect going on in my family, where now hardly any of that exists at all. It is also an excellent decision on my parents' part to have divorced when they did, instead of waiting a few years on my behalf. Being a very small child at the time of the divorce, I think, made the whole thing much less disturbing and unnerving as it would have been had I spent more of my early childhood thinking of my parents as two people meant to live together.

I've had friends ask me, when I'm leaving my mom's house to go to my dad's house, if I need to pack some clothes, shampoo, or anything for the next day. I feel slightly shocked whenever I am asked this, because the concept of one of my houses being more like home than the other is so alien to me. I've grown up equally in both houses, and both are thoroughly my home. At my dad's house, as at my mom's house, I keep my clothes, childhood toys, old school art projects, books and stuffed animals. I do not live separate lives when at the different houses, because both houses are marked in the same way by my transition from the 2-year-old to 14-year-old. I love that both houses are me now, and that each one has elements of all the stages of my life.

> *"A child's preference, even if clear and 'persistent' is not a change of circumstances warranting a modification."*

A Child's Preference May Not Influence a Change in Custody

The New Jersey Superior Court's Decision

Superior Court of New Jersey

In Traynor n/k/a Dallara v. Traynor *(2011), Gerard Traynor appealed the denial of his motion to change his twelve-year-old daughter's primary parent of residence based on her preference to live with him. In the following viewpoint, the Superior Court of New Jersey contends that a child's preference should not control the outcome of custody cases. The court also argues there were signs that Traynor attempted to pressure his daughter to live with him. Moreover, the child was doing well under the original custody arrangement, the court maintains, and modifying it was not in her best interest.*

Opinion, *Traynor n/k/a Dallara v. Traynor*, The Superior Court of New Jersey, Appellate Division, March 29, 2011.

Defendant Gerard Traynor appeals from the March 26, 2010 denial of his application to become the parent of primary residence (PPR) of the parties' then eleven-year-old daughter, and the award of $1530 in counsel fees to plaintiff Lisa M. Traynor, n/k/a Dallara. For the reasons that follow, we affirm.

The parties divorced on May 19, 2003. Since that time, they have sought post-judgment relief on at least twelve occasions. Six of these proceedings were before Judge [Michael J.] Haas, who rendered the decision now appealed. This was [the] defendant's third application to become PPR since 2008.

The child has expressed a preference to live with her father, although she currently does very well both in- and out-of-school. She enjoys a good relationship not only with her biological parents, but with her step-parents and her blended families. When the child was approximately eight years old, she was given the mistaken impression, by one or both of her parents, that she had the right to choose the home where she preferred to live. As Judge Haas found, however, there are indications [the] defendant may be unwittingly pressuring the child to live with him. An example of this conduct was his gift to the child of a backpack bearing the logo of the grade school in his district.

After [the] defendant's initial application in 2008, evaluations were completed and a parenting coordinator, Kim Fendrick, was appointed. Fendrick's summary [was] issued in May 2009.

The court's most important subsequent directive was that the parties and the child engage in counseling because, regardless of the outcome of the motions, they would need assistance in adjusting to the status quo, particularly the child. No such counseling has occurred.

On appeal, [the] defendant raises the following points:

> POINT I: JUDGE HAAS ABDICATED HIS ROLE AS PARENS PATRIAE

> POINT II: JUDGE HAAS ABUSED HIS DISCRETION BY INDICATING THAT INTERVIEWING WITH A 12 YEAR

OLD WOULD BE "SCARY" AND BY REFUSING TO CONDUCT THE INTERVIEW....

We affirm, essentially for the reasons stated in Judge Haas's thorough, detailed, and considered statements of reasons. We principally rely upon his factfinding and legal analysis, and make only the following brief comments.

The standard of review on matters of custody and parenting time is highly deferential. The conclusions of trial judges regarding child custody are "entitled to great weight and will not be lightly disturbed on appeal."

No Substantial Issue for an Interview

In his first two points, defendant asserts Judge Haas "abdicated his role" by refusing to interview the child. We do not agree. Rule 5:8–6 vests in the trial court only the discretion to interview a child if there is a genuine and substantial issue of custody. It does not impose a mandate. As defendant has not established changed

A child's preference on which parent to live with after a divorce is usually not taken into consideration by the courts, even when the child has a strong aversion to one parent. © Kevin Cooley/Getty Images.

circumstances since entry of the 2008 order, and as the only basis for his application is the child's continuing expressed wish, no genuine and substantial issue exists in the present case.

Defendant's reliance on *Mackowski v. Mackowski* [1998] . . . is misplaced. There, the court found an interview necessary in order to assess the real circumstances of the family, unfiltered by lawyers. The Rule change enacted since *Mackowski*, however, requires an interview only when the judge determines the circumstances compel it. The reasons for the amendment seem obvious: a child's stated preference should not be controlling . . . and, furthermore, such interviews can be quite emotionally damaging to a child.

The Child's Preference Does Not Warrant Modification

In any event, as Judge Haas explained in his March 26, 2010 decision,

> Defendant continues to point to what he describes as [the child's] "consistently expressed desire" to have him become the PPR. But, it is clear to the Court from the parties' certifications that defendant continues to engage the child in these discussions, to the point of giving her presents emblazoned with his local school's logo. [The child] is 11 years old. Obviously, at that young age, she responds to parental cues. While the Court cannot make a clear finding that defendant is attempting to pressure the child to live with him, it is very clear that he is continuing a campaign that began years ago when he, and plaintiff, first thought it would be a good idea to have the child decide where she should live. The October 2008 order found that, because of the parents' actions, [the child] was going to need counseling regardless of where she resided. Because [the child] was doing well under the current arrangement, that arrangement was kept in place. And, this arrangement will remain in place until there has been a significant change of circumstances that requires a modification in order to serve [the

I DON'T CARE WHICH PARENT I GET AS LONG AS IT'S THE SAME ONE THAT GETS THE PLAYSTATION.

"I don't care which parent I get as long as it's the same one that gets the Playstation," cartoon by John Martin. www.CartoonStock.com.

> child's] best interests. That is not the case here. What this family needs is counseling. They do not need constant litigation.

Judge Haas was well aware of the child's expressed wish, which no doubt would only be reiterated during an interview. Hopefully by the time of this writing, the parties and the child have become involved in therapy to assist everyone in adjusting to their current status.

In our view, Judge Haas's factual findings were amply warranted and entitled to the deference customarily given to such findings by the Family Part. His application of the relevant law was also correct. As he stated, "a child's preference, even if clear and 'persistent' is not a change of circumstances warranting a modification." His interpretation of the law, as applied to the facts of this case, reflects a judicious assessment of the family dynamics presented to him. We therefore do not agree that he abdicated his role as a judge, abused his discretion, or was required to interview the child or order a plenary hearing.

Viewpoint 12

> *"Increasing the role a child plays in custody decisions may well interfere with normal development and nudge the child into an unhealthy alliance with one parent."*

Allowing Teens to Address the Court in Custody Cases May Be Problematic

Leslie Ellen Shear

In the following viewpoint, an attorney argues that allowing teens to address the court in custody cases may not be in their best interest. Addressing a recently enacted statute in California, she maintains that reliably interviewing and obtaining accurate information from children and adolescents requires in-depth training and expertise, which most legal and court professionals lack. Moreover, the author continues, such direct participation may negatively impact the child, who may feel pressured to express a preference for one parent. However, the author also contends that vital information provided by children in court could greatly benefit the outcome of custody proceedings. Leslie Ellen Shear is a private practice attorney based in Encino, California.

Leslie Ellen Shear, "Dude, I'm 14 Years Old and I'm Here to Address the Court . . . Now What? California Prepares for Teenagers in Family Court," *IAML Law Journal*, vol. 4, Summer 2011.

In January 2012 California teenagers will begin exercising the right to "address the court" about their own custody under a newly enacted section of the state's Family Code. California's family courts are preparing for this change, ruminating about how it will work in practice, and wondering whether it will create a court culture that ends up with greater direct involvement of younger children as well. The practical questions begin with how teenagers (who generally aren't reading the California Family Code) learn that they have a right to address the court, and include questions about the quality of information judges will obtain, and the short and long-term impact on children of participating in custody litigation.

What do the parties, lawyers and judges hope to learn from children's direct participation in custody proceedings? The new statute (and its enabling court rule) fail to distinguish between three very different purposes for a child's direct participation. Those possible purposes for direct child-involvement are:

1. Factual testimony by the child as a percipient witness;
2. The child addresses the court [to] express preferences about the prospective parenting plan; or
3. The Court meeting the child for purposes of learning about the child's unique traits and characteristics as they bear on provisions of the parenting plan. . . .

Questions and Concerns

The new legislation increasing the likelihood of children's direct involvement in custody litigation raises many questions and concerns. A number of those who commented on the proposed rule opposed its adoption, but the Administrative Office of the Courts correctly observed that the California Legislature has mandated adoption of enabling rules. Comments noted the lack of funding to properly implement this new program—the new statute is an unfunded mandate.

Many California family law professionals wonder and worry about the impact on children of direct participation in litigation about their family relationships. In the current family court setting, this new policy is likely to produce decontextualized information that sheds little light on which parenting plan is in a particular child's best interests or accurate information about events the child has witnessed.

In *The Moral Intelligence of Children: How to Raise a Moral Child* (Random House, 1997), psychiatrist Robert Coles tells us how he learned something important from his young son. One day Dr. Coles' son slipped away and played with his father's power tools—suffering a severe cut. Dr. Coles put him in the car and took off for the emergency room. In his anxiety to get there quickly he started running yellow lights until the boy said, "Daddy, I think we are going to get in more trouble trying to get out of trouble." Will increasing children's direct participation in family law litigation create more trouble than it prevents? The risks seem higher in the current setting, where courts are carrying heavier caseloads, resources for court-connected mental health services are shrinking, and job instability may prevent many parents from obtaining counsel.

When the statute creating a large role for children in family court courtrooms was first adopted, some thought family courts would turn to child protection (dependency courts) for models about how to implement the statute. But the differences between the two courts are more significant than the similarities. One bench officer who came to family law from years as a dependency court lawyer, and a dependency court commissioner observes that unlike children who testify in dependency court, children in family court go home that night with a parent or parents who may not be pleased with what the child had to say, or may reward the child for supporting the parent's goals and perspectives. Thus, children's involvement in family court presents different questions about the influences on what the child has to say, and the consequences for the child after the proceedings.

To reflect upon how best to decide when and how teenagers will address family courts, we will return to the purposes for which a child's participation in custody litigation process could be used, the ways in which California family law courts can learn what the child has to say, the reliability and quality of different ways of obtaining information, and the question of iatrogenic consequences of the child's direct involvement in courtroom proceedings over the child's custody. We also consider the impact of direct involvement on the child, and the skills and methods necessary to get reliable and useful information.

Since the phrase "address the court" is fairly ambiguous, individual family law judges may have considerable latitude in implement this new law. The new statute refers to the child

Many argue that giving a child the right to address the court in regards to their own custody may not be in the child's best interest. © Glow Images/Getty Images.

expressing a preference or providing "other input regarding custody or visitation" but doesn't make it clear whether the child is a witness subject to cross-examination; a quasi-party to the litigation seeking or opposing orders from the court; or is making something akin to a victim's statement in criminal court proceedings. Similarly, it is unclear whether the Legislature intended the teenager to be testifying about facts, voicing opinions, or offering an opportunity for the Court to get to know the child whose custody is at issue. The new court rules suggest a variety of approaches by which family courts can hear from children. . . .

Developing Best Practices for Teenagers to Address Family Courts

Family law judges, lawyers and mental health professionals in California are speculating about how they will practice under the new statute and court rules—and trying to get ready. Decisions about when and how the new law will be applied turn on a complex set of questions.

Why is this teenager addressing the court? Is the teenager appearing as an advocate for himself or herself, a percipient witness to relevant facts, or so the court has some sense of the traits of the individual whose parenting plan is being developed? The new court rule fails to distinguish between these purposes, but practitioners and bench officers should bring a higher level of rigor to consideration of this question. In this arena, form will follow function—surely we can't decide how the child will participate until we clarify the purpose of this child's participation.

How does the teenager learn that the right to address the court exists? Should parents, lawyers, or family court professionals be inviting young people to address the court? Should they be discussing the proposed parenting plans at-issue, or letting the teenager know about the legal and factual questions being considered by the court? Should lawyers be interviewing the teenagers as prospective witnesses? Do the parents have a due process right to discover (by deposition or other means) what the teenager has to say? What about cross-examination? What impact will it have on teenagers to treat them as part of a parent's litigation team against the other parent?

The new rule requires minors' counsel, child custody evaluators, recommending counselors and other court-connected professionals to advise the Court "if they have information that" the child wants to be heard. The rule permits parties and parties' lawyers to do so. It is not clear whether any of these professionals have a duty to advise the teenager of this right, or whether they are to wait until the child expresses a wish to communicate with the court.

How should this teenager address the court? Does the teen address the court through a monologue from the witness stand, by letter or declaration, through a lawyer or mental health intermediary? Should the court interview this teenager in chambers. If so, on or off the record? Who else should be present? How will questions for the teen be crafted? What about follow-up questions? The proposed rules permit a wide range of options, including employing a mental health professional to conduct a child interview (thereby obtaining decontextualized data), or allowing a judge to interview the child in chambers accompanied only by a court reporter (thus placing the highly skilled task of forensic interviewing in the hands of a person without in-depth training, and depriving the parents of the opportunity for cross-examination). In most cases where there is important information to obtain from the child, a child custody evaluation will be the best option. Unfortunately, limited economic resources may lead to use of less-effective options.

How does the child's participation in contested litigation differ from the child's participation in custody mediation, collaborative divorce negotiations, or other forms of Consensual Dispute Resolution (CDR)? We know from the research that teenagers have a strong interest in helping plan their schedules in light of their school, enrichment and social activities. But is consulting in that process when parents are working on an agreement materially different than when parents presenting evidence and a judge is making the decisions?

What sense will the decision makers make of the decontextualized information they get from the teenager's statement? When is it not in the teenager's best interests to address the court? What training do professionals need to interview or take testimony from teenagers in custody cases, and what training do they need to interpret what the teen has to say? How does the teenage brain differ from the adult brain? How stable are this teen's views—and how realistic are they? How accurate [are] this teen's accounts of events and relationships?

What impact will direct participation have on the child and the family? Will the child be over-empowered, with parents engaging in permissive parenting because they fear loss of custody? Will their parental authority be compromised? Will the child be anxious about the experience, feel trapped in the middle, or subjected to intolerable pressures to express a preference for one parent, or adopt that parent's views about events and relationships? Will the child feel guilty in the future about picking a parent? Will the parents' express their hurt or anger to the child when they learn the content of the child's remarks, or when the parenting plan doesn't reflect their desires. Will the child regret decisions based upon an unrealistic view about what life with the other parent will actually look like? Will the child request multiple opportunities to address the court as his or her preferences and experiences change?

A Challenging Experiment

One of the things social psychology research teaches us is that once a person takes a public position, that individual becomes wedded to that position. Children and adolescents naturally gravitate to different parents over the course of childhood. Inviting the child to state a preference in the course of litigation interrupts those natural experiences and freezes the child into what might well otherwise be a temporary perception as the

About one in six custodial parents are fathers.

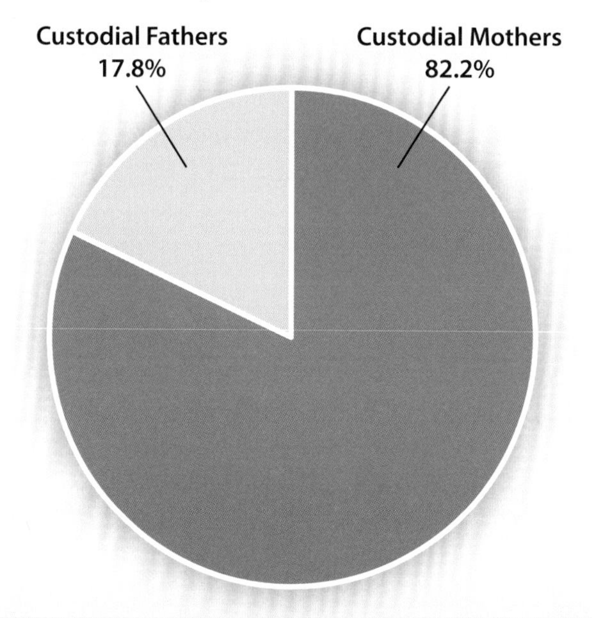

Taken From: US Census Bureau, "Custodial Mothers and Fathers and Their Child Support," December 2011.

young person individuates, and develops his or her own identity. Thus increasing the role a child plays in custody decisions may well interfere with normal development and nudge the child into an unhealthy alliance with one parent to the exclusion or minimization of the relationship with the other parent.

These decisions must be educated, informed, individualized decisions. It takes a great deal of expertise to make wise policy decisions about involving children in the court process, and about whether and how to involve a particular child or adolescent. Most family judges, and lawyers, and many mental health professionals simply do not have the training and experience to avoid doing harm.

Few professionals have sufficient training in interviewing children, understanding the growing research about the strengths and limitations of children's memory, intellectual development, and thinking, or in integrating the data they get directly from children with the other information in the case to make informed decisions about the parenting plan. Brief trainings do not suffice—competent forensic interviewing of children requires extensive training that includes supervised forensic interviewing in a clinical setting. It is important to note that training to work with children as a therapist or diagnostician is very different from training to interview children for investigative and forensic purposes....

California has begun a challenging experiment to incorporate children's perspectives into the development of their parenting plans at a time where it lacks the resources to provide the kind of safeguards family law professionals view as essential. It is likely that the state's family courts will be engaging in a lot of trial and error as they attempt to implement the new statute and court rule.

13

Viewpoint

> *"In reality, a custody agreement that meets the needs of a toddler is unlikely to be right for a teenager."*

Custody Orders and Children's Changing Needs

Ruth Bettelheim

In the following viewpoint, a family therapist argues that custody orders do not meet the needs of children, which change as they enter adolescence. Arrangements and schedules are developed and maintained in ways that govern children's daily lives until they turn eighteen, and parents are highly reluctant to revisit the terms, the author alleges. Consequently, she proposes that the following be included in the custody process: parenting plans are reviewed every two years, children speak privately with mediation-trained lawyers, and children's wishes are prioritized over those of experts and judges. Ruth Bettelheim is a marriage and family therapist.

In divorced families, whose needs count for more: those of parents or those of children?

When parents divorce, their child custody plans are supposed to place the "best interests of the child" first. We know children's needs change as they grow. Unfortunately, the way we develop and maintain custody schedules ignores that, and often makes children feel helpless by denying them any influence over the arrangements that govern their lives.

Today, most divorces involving children include a parenting plan that dictates where children will live and which days they will spend with each parent. The process of agreeing on a custody arrangement is often very difficult for parents, who naturally have little desire to revisit the divorce experience. As a result, the legal agreement they reach typically will govern the daily rhythm and schedule of children without change until they turn 18.

In reality, a custody agreement that meets the needs of a toddler is unlikely to be right for a teenager. Imagine yourself as a 13-year-old who wants to spend more time with your friends over the weekends. Unfortunately, your parents are divorced, and you spend weekends with a parent who lives two hours away. You would be unlikely to request a change in custody because it would mean altering a longstanding agreement and plunging into a morass of conflicting loyalties and guilt over betraying whichever parent would lose out. Faced with such dilemmas, children in divorced families frequently end up suppressing their own needs to reduce conflict with, or between, their parents. Even when children are driven to speak up and request custody modifications, their voices carry little, if any, legal weight.

Children Deserve a Voice in the Process

Rendering children voiceless and powerless to meet their own changing needs, or burdening them with guilt if they try to do so, is in no one's best interest. It either creates hardship for children who grin and bear it or instigates a string of provocative and damaging behaviors in those who embark on increasingly desperate attempts to make someone notice that something is wrong.

Custody arrangements made when children are toddlers may create friction and dilemmas for them as they grow up and their needs evolve. © David Seed Photography/Getty Images.

Although the United Nations Convention on the Rights of the Child states that children have a right to meaningful participation in decisions affecting them, adults, from some misguided notion of protection, often seek to keep children from making choices in custody matters. But accepting certain kinds of responsibility for their own lives and learning from the consequences of their decisions, even poor ones, is vital for the growth and well-being of all children.

Once children have reached the age of reason—generally agreed to be about 7—they should be recognized as the ultimate experts on their own lives. We all resent it when others say that they know better than we do how we feel and what is good for us. Nevertheless, we subject children to this when we call in experts to evaluate their lives over a period of days or weeks, as part of the custody process, instead of just listening to them.

Recognizing Children's Rights

To remedy this, all parenting plans should be subjected to mandatory binding review every two years. The review should include a forum for children to speak privately with a mediation-trained lawyer. The conversation should be recorded to ensure that the child was not pressured or asked leading questions. Children should not be forced to state preferences but invited to speak if they choose. Many children will decline, as they are deeply reluctant to hurt a parent. But occasionally, the need to advocate

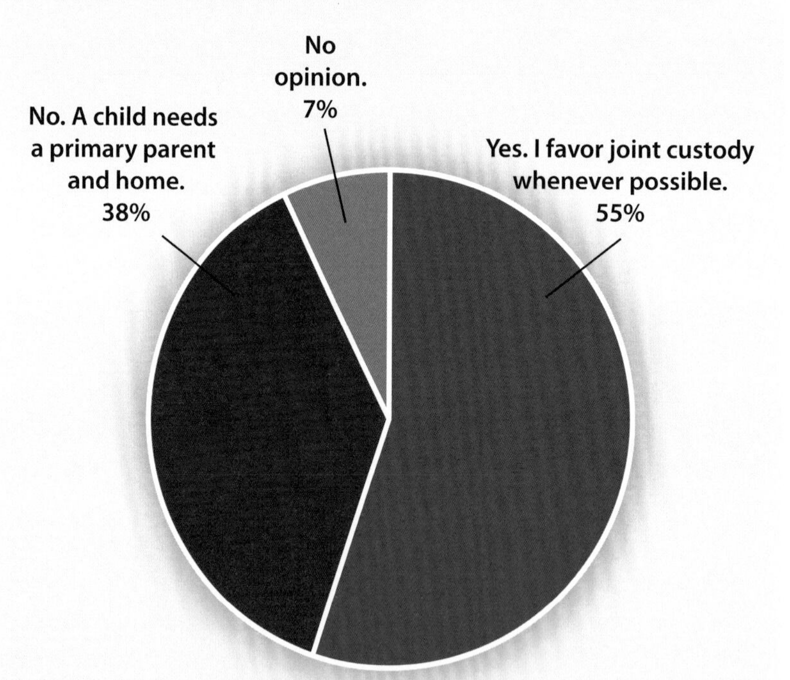

Taken From: FamilyEducation.com, Divorce and Joint Custody poll results, life.familyeducation.com.

for themselves outweighs these fears. When they do speak up, their wishes should be honored as stated, not as interpreted by an expert or lawyer.

The lawyer should meet with all family members, individually and as a group, to ensure that the child's wishes are respected in the next two-year parenting plan. Children's wishes should be decisive, in place of those of experts and judges, as long as at least one parent agrees with them.

Some may fear this system would result in young children being manipulated by their parents. But my almost 40 years of practice as a family and child therapist have taught me several things that suggest otherwise. First, that children can tell the difference between being bribed and manipulated, and being respected, understood and having their needs (including those for discipline) met. Second, that children consistently choose the latter over the former, if given the chance. And finally, that children have a clear understanding of their own needs—even if they are unable to articulate justifications or reasons for their wishes.

Of course, even after listening to children, the success of custody plans must still be evaluated. A proper assessment of children includes their functioning at home, at school and in having age-appropriate peer relationships. If, after following a modified custody plan for two years, a child is failing in two of the three areas, then it is time to consider whether a different plan is needed.

In 1970, no-fault divorce made its first [well-known] appearance in the United States, in California, bringing recognition that both parents have an equal right to have access to their children. Forty years later, in 2010, New York became the last state to adopt no-fault divorce. But children's rights are still routinely ignored. Will it take another 40 years for children to be heard?

14

Viewpoint

> *"The entire divorce regime is nothing less than a massive assault on every major principle of the U.S. Constitution."*

Divorce and Custody Orders Violate the Rights of Parents

Stephen Baskerville

In the following viewpoint, a government professor contends that divorce and custody orders are forms of government interference that infringe upon constitutional rights by dissolving private households and separating parents from children. As a result of the divorce revolution, the author maintains, legal authority over children has been transferred to family courts, which regularly remove parents from homes—particularly fathers—who have committed no wrongdoing. Furthermore, the courts in many cases have restricted the religious, political, and civic expressions of adults in the parent-child relationship, he asserts. Stephen Baskerville is an assistant professor of government at Patrick Henry College, president of the American Coalition for Fathers and Children, and author of Taken Into Custody: The War Against Fathers, Marriage, and the Family.

Stephen Baskerville, *Taken Into Custody: The War Against Fathers, Marriage, and the Family.* Nashville: Cumberland House, 2007, pp. 75–83.

Advocates of unilateral divorce often portray it as a "liberating experience" and claim it is a "citizen's right" and even a "civil liberty." Yet when children are involved, it is no exaggeration to say that the regime of involuntary divorce has become the most authoritarian institution in our society today.

Contrary to general assumption, divorce today involves much more than spouses simply deciding to part ways. While divorce is often considered a "private" matter, and therefore immune from the scrutiny of scholars, journalists, and the public, it raises fundamental questions about the government's role in private life. Far more than marriage, divorce by its nature requires active government intervention. Marriage creates a private household, which may or may not necessitate signing some legal documents. Divorce dissolves a private household, usually against the wishes of one spouse. It inevitably involves the state—including police and prisons—to enforce the divorce and the post-marriage order. Otherwise, one spouse might continue to claim the protections and prerogatives of private life: the right to live in the common home, to possess the common property, or—most vexing of all—to parent the common children.

Few people stopped to consider the implications of laws that shifted the breakup of private households from a voluntary to an involuntary process. If marriage is not a wholly private affair, involuntary divorce by its nature requires constant supervision over private life by state officials. Unilateral divorce, by its very nature, inescapably involves government agents evicting people from their homes, confiscating their property, and separating them from their children. Far from being a private matter, it inherently denies not only the inviolability of marriage but the very concept of a private sphere of life.

Proceeding from this, no-fault divorce introduced novel concepts into the legal system, such as the principle that one could be decreed guilty of violating an agreement that one had, in fact, not violated. "According to therapeutic precepts, the fault for marital breakup must be shared, even when one spouse unilaterally seeks a divorce," observes author Barbara Whitehead. "Many husbands and wives who did not seek or want divorce were stunned to learn . . . that they were equally 'at fault' in the dissolution of their marriages."

A Rise in Government Intervention

The "fault" that was ostensibly thrown out the front door of divorce proceedings re-entered through the back, but now without precise definition. The judiciary was expanded from its traditional role of punishing crime or tort to punishing personal imperfections and private differences: suddenly, one could be summoned to court without having committed any legal infraction; the verdict was pre-determined before any evidence was examined; and one could be found "guilty" of things that were not illegal. "Lawmakers eliminated a useful inquiry process and replaced it with an automatic outcome," writes Judy Parejko, author of *Stolen Vows*. "No other court process is so devoid of recourse for a defendant. When one spouse files for divorce, his/her spouse is automatically found 'guilty' of irreconcilable differences and is not allowed a defense."

The "automatic outcome" quickly expanded into what effectively became a presumption of guilt against the forcibly divorced spouse ("defendant"). The very involvement of the judiciary, with its handmaid, the penal apparatus—machinery ordinarily reserved for punishing criminal or civil wrongdoing—indicates how marriage dissolution blurs distinctions our justice system was previously at pains to delineate carefully: private versus public, civil versus criminal, therapy versus justice, sin versus crime. When government stopped enforcing the marriage contract it began enforcing the divorce decree. The result was not the removal of the state from family life but an explosion of extensive and intrusive governmental instruments whose sole purpose is intervention in families. Once again, the leverage comes through children.

Intruding upon the Rights of Parents

The right of parents to raise and care for their children without interference by the state has long been recognized by the Supreme Court and other federal courts as among the most fundamental rights of American citizens. Numerous judicial decisions have held that parenthood is an "essential" right, that "undeniably warrants deference, and, absent a powerful countervailing interest, protection." Parenthood "cannot be denied without violating those fundamental principles of liberty and justice which lie at the base of all our civil and political institutions." Parental rights have been characterized by the courts as "sacred" and "inherent, natural right[s], for the protection of which, just as much as for the protection of the rights of the individual to life, liberty, and the pursuit of happiness, our government is formed."

A substantial body of federal case law recognizes parenting as a "liberty interest," a basic constitutional right protected under the Fourteenth Amendment: "The liberty interest and the integrity of the family encompass an interest in retaining custody of one's children, and thus a state may not interfere with a parent's custodial right absent due process protections." A federal court has held that "the parent-child relationship is a liberty interest protected by the due process clause of the Fourteenth Amendment." Likewise, a parent's "right to the care, custody, management and companionship of [his or her] minor children" is an interest "far more precious than . . . property rights." [U.S. Supreme Court] Justice Thurgood Marshall wrote in another case, "We have recognized on numerous occasions that the relationship between parent and child is constitutionally protected," and "a (once) married father who is separated or divorced from a mother and is no longer living with his child" could not be treated differently from a father who is married and still living with his child.

As recently as 2000, the Supreme Court has reiterated that "parental rights are absolute": "The liberty interest at issue . . . the interest of parents in the care, custody, and control of their children—is perhaps the oldest of the fundamental liberty interests recognized by this Court.... [I]t cannot now be doubted that the Due Process Clause of the Fourteenth Amendment protects the fundamental right of parents to make decisions concerning the care, custody, and control of their children."

I labor this point somewhat because the current practice of family courts is to act as if such precedents simply do not exist. One might expect these apparently unequivocal constitutional principles would be clear and strong enough to protect the rights of parents and their children not to be arbitrarily separated. Yet they are simply ignored in cases of involuntary divorce. It is not difficult to see why. The age-old principle stipulating, in the words of Supreme Court Justice Byron White, a "realm of family life which the state cannot enter" is a direct threat to the raison d'etre [reason for existence] of family courts, whose very existence is predicated on the principle that no realm of life is too private for the intervention of the government.

Before the divorce revolution and the rise of family courts, legal authority over children had long been recognized to reside with their parents. "For centuries it has been a canon of law that parents speak for their minor children," wrote [U.S. Supreme Court] Justice Potter Stewart. "So deeply embedded in our traditions is this principle of the law the Constitution itself may compel a state to respect it." We have already seen that family courts have transferred from parents to themselves the authority to determine what is best for children, to the point where they routinely rule that the "best interest" of children lies in removing them from parents who have done nothing wrong and appointing lawyers to speak for children against their parents. Here too the new courts can be seen to be directly antithetical to ancient traditions and precedents of common law, for the very existence of family court proceeds from the principle that "the child's best interest is perceived as being independent of the parents, and a court review is held to be necessary to protect the child's interests."

Criminalizing Parenthood

The implications extend far beyond family law. A very fundamental shift has taken place here in the power of government over private life, without the slightest opposition or even notice. If parents do not have ultimate control over their children (absent some legally recognized transgression by which they forfeit it), they effectively have no private lives, and government becomes total. Parents who resist the government's assumption of control over their children—not necessarily by open defiance but simply by exercising the ordinary acts of parenthood—become criminals, and those acts of parenthood, such as being with your children and making decisions about them, become criminal acts. Parenthood itself is criminalized.

Courts generally grant fewer custody and visitation rights to fathers. Critics say that this type of court interference in family relationships is a clear infringement of constitutional rights. © Image Source/Getty Images.

While parents generally are the principal impediments to the expanding power of the courts, and while mothers also fall afoul of family court judges, it is the father whose presence constitutes an intact family and against whom the enmity of the judges is largely directed. In fact, it is no exaggeration to say that the existence of family courts, and virtually every issue they adjudicate—divorce, custody, child abuse, child-support enforcement, even adoption and juvenile crime—depend upon one overriding principle: remove the father. So long as fathers remain with their families, family courts have little reason to exist, since the problems they handle seldom arise in intact families. The power to remove the father is the cardinal power of family court.

This comes out, somewhat inadvertently, in a three-part investigative series in the *Observer* newspaper depicting behavior typical of family court judges. "The reasons given in reports as to why a father's access should be restricted or denied often seem arbitrary, to put it mildly," the newspaper comments. Any rationalization is clearly adequate; just get the father out:

> One applicant had cancer which . . . "could be upsetting" for his child. A man might be said to "lack sensitivity" or be "over-enthusiastic" or even "father-centered"—for which tendency one man was denied all contact with his child. In one case, it was noted disapprovingly that a father had told his son he preferred Scrabble to Monopoly and thought hyacinths smelled sweeter than roses. This was seen as "taking the lead in contact"—a form of emotional abuse, according to the reporting officer. One father wore a black shirt, which "could be intimidating." Another stood accused of "losing his temper with customs officials in a French airport" . . . and was therefore said to have an "unfortunate disposition." One report could find no reason why a child should not see more of his father but went on to conclude: "Nonetheless, the mother must be concerned about something." The father's contact was limited to two hours every six weeks.

The Power of the Family Court

For all the outpouring of concern about the family and judicial power in recent years, it is strange that so little attention is ever focused on the institution where the two meet: family courts. This is especially strange when one considers that the crisis of the family has coincided with a marked erosion of public respect for the legal profession and a widespread belief that the judiciary has assumed powers it was never intended to have. Family courts are without question the arm of the state that routinely reaches farthest into the private lives of individuals and families. The very idea of a "family" court—whose rulings are enforced by plainclothes officials who amount to family police—should alert us to danger. Yet far from scrutinizing these tribunals, we give them virtually unchecked power. Shrouded in secrecy and leaving no record of their proceedings, they are accountable to virtually no one. "The family court is the most powerful branch of the judiciary," according to Robert Page, presiding judge of the Family Part of the Superior Court of New Jersey. By their own assessment, writes Page, "the power of family court judges is almost unlimited."

Predictably, with unlimited power, these courts are out of control. The eminent Roscoe Pound once observed that "the powers of the Star Chamber were a trifle in comparison with those of our juvenile court and courts of domestic relations." The lowest and least prestigious sector of Alexander Hamilton's "least dangerous branch" of government, family courts routinely separate children from parents who have done nothing wrong, ignore due process of law, and even silence political dissent.

"Michigan courts do not provide a fair, or impartial, tribunal for any domestic relations litigant," says one attorney. "Instead, they customarily and regularly deprive litigants of due process of law." As Pound indicates, these courts now occupy a place in our political system reminiscent of the dreaded "prerogative" courts of High Commission and Star Chamber in seventeenth-century England or the notorious chancery court in the nineteenth century. Malcolm X once described family court as "modern slavery," and Supreme Court Justice Abe Fortas characterized them with the term "kangaroo court."

Though the system for adjudicating family law is different in each jurisdiction, the essential pattern is similar. Family courts describe themselves as courts of "equity" (or more pretentiously, "chancery") rather than "law." Strikingly, they do not consider themselves necessarily bound by due process of law, including the Bill of Rights; nor are the rules of evidence as stringent as in criminal courts. As one father reports being told by the chief investigator for the administrator of the courts in New Jersey, investigating a complaint of judicial wrongdoing: "The provisions of the U.S. Constitution do not apply in domestic relations cases since they are determined in a court of equity rather than a court of law."

The Eleventh Amendment to the Constitution has been interpreted by judges to render themselves immune from lawsuits, and they are protected from federal oversight by the "domestic relations exception," a blanket refusal by federal courts to review any case involving family law, even when it includes violations of fundamental constitutional rights. As we have seen, family courts are accountable only to review boards dominated by bar associations.

Family courts usually operate behind closed doors and generally do not record their proceedings. Ostensibly the secrecy is to protect the family privacy of litigants, though more often it has precisely the opposite effect: The secrecy provides a cloak not to protect privacy but to invade it with impunity. "Is it possible," asks columnist Al Knight with reference to legislation that would automatically seal all family court records, "that the district court judges, divorce lawyers, special advocates and guardians *ad litem* [guardian for the purpose of the suit], and a cadre of social workers might simply like less public attention paid to their activities?"

The courts having successfully asserted the power to remove children from legally innocent parents, other violations of basic constitutional rights and civil liberties flow logically—and almost inexorably, much as one lie necessitates another. The entire divorce regime is nothing less than a massive assault on every major principle of the U.S. Constitution. One can run point by point down the Bill of Rights and other articles, and there is hardly one that is not routinely violated by family courts.

Prohibiting Parental Expression

First Amendment guarantees of freedom of expression and religion have long been understood to include parents' relationships with their children. Yet family court judges routinely control what parents may say and do with their children, including what religious worship they may or must attend and what they may discuss in private, as well as what they may say about their legal case in public.

A 1997 ruling of the Massachusetts Supreme Court prohibiting a father from taking his children to Christian services received some media attention but no opposition from either churches or civil libertarians. In Arlington, Virginia, a judge's 1997 injunction prohibiting a father from taking his son to Bar Mitzvah was reversed only after a protest in front of the county courthouse. The father's attorney, Charles Janus, called the order "a violation of the First Amendment right to freedom of religion" and due process. In Arkansas, a father is ordered to take his child to the church of the mother's choice during his visitation time. A vegetarian father in Arlington shows a court order preventing him from discussing "diet" with his children. A Missouri father cannot take his son to political meetings. An Arizona father is "restrained and enjoined from discussing with [his sixteen-year-old daughter] his claims that the attorneys involved in the case, and any judge that has been involved in the case, have acted improperly or in an illegal manner," reads one court order. "They are not to be discussed."

These are not isolated incidents. "The best interests test leaves courts free to make custody decisions based on parents' speech, and to issue orders restricting their speech," writes law professor Eugene Volokh. "This willingness of courts to disfavor a broad range of parental ideologies . . . atheist or fundamentalist, racist or pro-polygamist, pro-homosexual or anti-homosexual—should lead us to take a hard look at the doctrine that allows

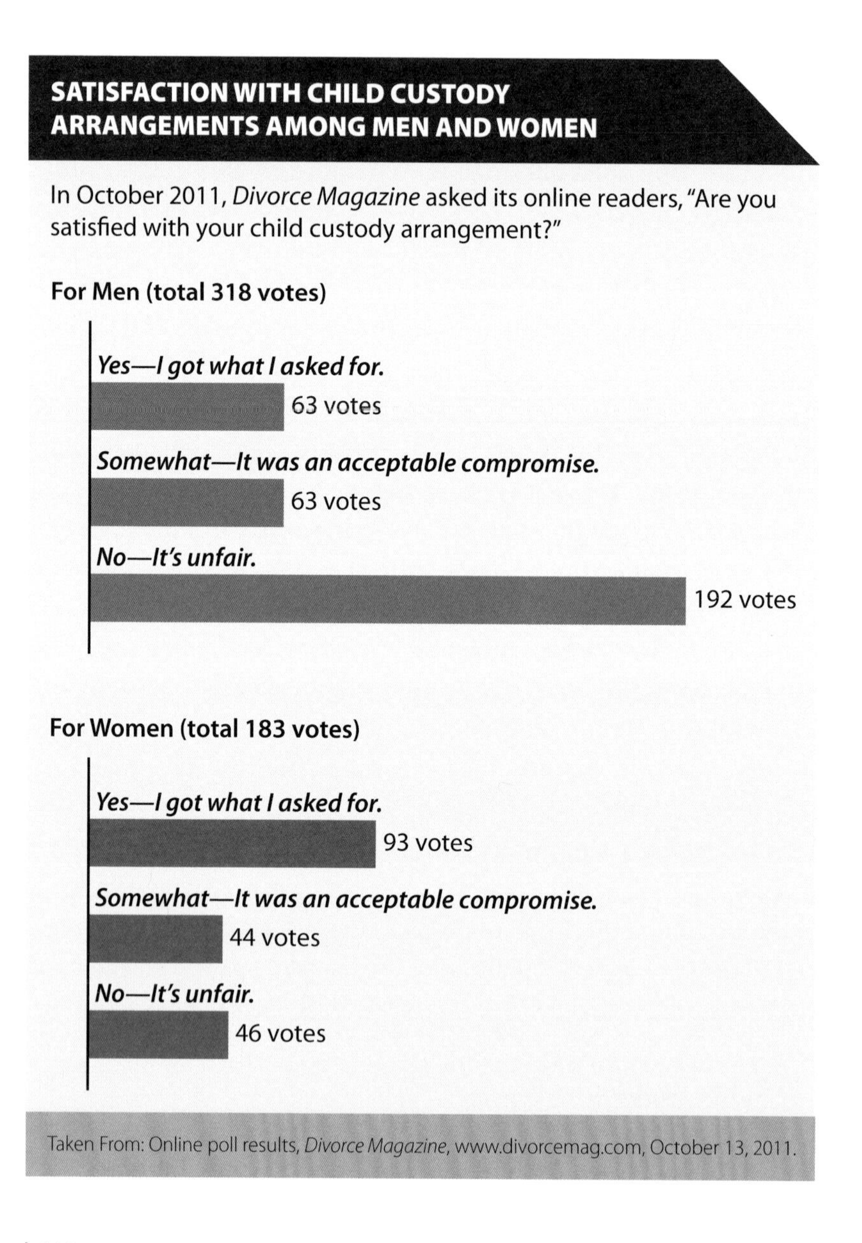

such results." Volokh documents how routine practices and rulings issued in family courts throughout America stand in direct violation of First Amendment protections and control intimate details of citizens' private lives: "Courts have . . . ordered parents to reveal their homosexuality to their children, or to conceal it. They have ordered parents not to swear in front of their children, and to install Internet filters. They have also considered, as a factor in the custody decision, parents' swearing, exposing their children to R-rated movies, a gun-themed magazine, unfiltered Internet access, photos of men in women's clothing, music with vulgar sexual content, and pornography."

Children as Hostages

All this is justified under the "best interests of the child" standard, which "leaves family court judges ample room to consider a parent's ideology":

> One parent, for instance, was ordered to "make sure that there is nothing in the religious upbringing or teaching that the minor child is exposed to that can be considered homophobic," because the other parent was homosexual. Parents have had their rights reduced based, in part, on their having told their children that the other parent was destined for damnation, or otherwise criticizing the other parent's religion. A court could likewise restrict a father's teaching his children that women must be subservient to men, since such speech might undermine the mother's authority.

Under the guise of protecting children from their own parents, the courts use the children as hostages to control the political expression of adults. "Many parents who know that certain speech might make a difference in their custody battles are likely to be deterred by this risk," writes Volokh. "Risk-averse parents may be deterred even by small risks, especially when the harm (loss of custody) is so grave."

Parents' attempts to educate their children in their own beliefs and instill in them religious or civic values are prohibited by family court judges. "Courts have restricted a parent's religious speech when such speech was seen as inconsistent with the religious education that the custodial parent was providing. The cases generally rest on the theory . . . that the children will be made confused and unhappy by the contradictory teachings, and will be less likely to take their parents' authority seriously," writes Volokh. "In one case . . . a court ordered 'that each party will impress upon the children the need for religious tolerance and not permit any third party to attempt to teach them otherwise.'"

So forced divorce allows officials the power to prohibit parents from confusing their children. Courts also prohibit parents from telling children of court orders restricting what they can tell them, "on the theory that such discussions are likely to remind the children about tension between the parents, or are likely to be accompanied by explicit or implied criticism of the other parent."

Once again, lest it be argued that parents necessarily surrender certain freedoms when they decide to divorce, parents who have not agreed to a divorce or who vigorously oppose it can still be stripped of these protections. "Child custody speech restrictions may be imposed on a parent even when the family's unity was abrogated by the other parent," Volokh observes. "The law here doesn't distinguish the leaving parent from the one who gets left." In other words, a law-abiding citizen minding his own business loses his First Amendment protections the moment his spouse files for divorce, without legal grounds, and turns the children over to government control.

Further, even divorce may not be necessary for the government to monitor and prohibit parental expression. "The law almost never restricts parental speech in intact families," Volokh notes. "You are free to teach your child racism, Communism, or the propriety of adultery or promiscuity. Judges won't decide whether your teachings confuse the child, cause him nightmares, or risk molding him into an immoral person. Judges won't enjoin the speech, or transfer custody to other people whose teachings will be more in the child's best interest." Yet this realm may also be threatened. "It's not clear that ideological restrictions limited to child custody disputes will stay limited," Volokh adds. "The government sometimes wants to interfere with parents' teaching their children even when there is no dispute between parents. . . . Many of the arguments supporting child custody speech restrictions . . . would also apply to restrictions imposed on intact families."

Organizations to Contact

The editors have compiled the following list of organizations concerned with the issues debated in this book. The descriptions are derived from materials provided by the organizations. All have publications or information available for interested readers. The list was compiled on the date of publication of the present volume; the information provided here may change. Be aware that many organizations take several weeks or longer to respond to inquiries, so allow as much time as possible.

American Coalition for Fathers and Children (ACFC)
1718 M Street NW, #187
Washington, DC 20036
(800) 978-3237
e-mail: info@acfc.org
website: www.acfc.org

ACFC advocates the creation of a family law system, legislative system, and public awareness that promotes equal rights for fathers affected by divorce, the breakup of a family, or establishment of paternity. The organization's website offers articles and information about divorce geared toward fathers.

Association of Family and Conciliation Courts (AFCC)
6525 Grand Teton Plaza
Madison, WI 53719
(608) 664-3750 • fax: (608) 664-3751
e-mail: afcc@afccnet.org
website: www.afccnet.org

The AFCC is an international association of judges, lawyers, counselors, custody evaluators, and mediators. The organization maintains a library of videos, pamphlets, and other publications on custody and visitation issues, child support, mediation, and more. The organization also sponsors parent education programs and conferences on a wide range of child welfare issues.

Child Welfare League of America (CWLA)

1726 M Street NW, Suite 500
Washington, DC 20036
(202) 688-4200 • fax: (202) 833-1689
website: www.cwla.org

Founded in 1920, CWLA is a membership-based child welfare organization. Its primary objective is to make children a national priority by providing direct support to agencies that serve children and families. In addition to sponsoring annual conferences and providing consultation services to child welfare agencies, the organization regularly publishes various materials concerning child welfare issues, including a bimonthly online magazine, *Children's Voice*, and the journal *Child Welfare.*

Children's Rights Council (CRC)

9470 Annapolis Road, Suite 310
Lanham, MD 20706
(301) 559-3120
e-mail: info@crckids.org
website: www.crckids.org

CRC is a non-profit organization that serves divorced, never-married, and extended families and at-risk youth. CRC promotes a society where laws, attitudes, and public opinion affirm that "The Best Parent is Both Parents." The council's mission is to minimize emotional, physical, and economic abuse; the neglect and distress of children; and the development of at-risk behaviors following relationship breakups between parents involved in highly conflicted marital disputes. CRC works to assure a child frequent, meaningful, and continuing contact with two parents and the extended family the child would normally have during a marriage.

Concerned Women for America (CWA)

1015 Fifteenth Street NW, Suite 1100
Washington, DC 20005
(202) 488-7000 • fax: (202) 488-0806
website: www.cwfa.org

CWA is an educational and legal defense foundation that seeks to strengthen the traditional family by employing Christian principles. In addition to providing a collection of the latest research and news concerning the maintenance of the nuclear family, the CWA publishes the monthly magazine *Family Voice* and offers various brochures and pamphlets.

Kids' Turn

1242 Market Street, 2nd Floor
San Francisco, CA 94102
(415) 777-9977 • fax: (415) 777-1577
e-mail: kidsturn@earthlink.net
website: http://kidsturn.org

Kids' Turn is a non-profit organization that helps children understand and cope with the loss, anger, and fear that often accompany separation or divorce. The organization also helps parents understand what support their children need during this crisis in their lives, so that at-risk behavior by children is averted. Kids' Turn is dedicated to enhancing the lives of these children through improved communication and the knowledge they are not alone. It publishes a blog on the *Huffington Post.*

National Family Resiliency Center (NFRC)

Century Plaza, Suite 121
Columbia, MD 21044
(301) 384-0079 • fax: (301) 596-1677
website: www.nfrchelp.org

NFRC provides parents and professionals with programs and resources to help them navigate the emotionally challenging process of separation, divorce, and remarriage. The center helps children better understand and accept the realities of life-changing experiences in their family and provides the guidance they need to identify and express their feelings in a healthy way.

National Youth Rights Association (NYRA)

1101 Fifteenth Street NW, Suite 200
Washington, DC 20005
(202) 835-1739
website: www.youthrights.org

NYRA is a youth-led national non-profit organization dedicated to fighting for the civil rights and liberties of young people. NYRA has members in all fifty states—more than seven thousand in total—and chapters from coast to coast. It offers an online forum on youth rights at home, covering topics such as parental authority and emancipation.

Nemours

10140 Centurion Pkwy.
Jacksonville, FL 32256
(904) 697-4100
website: http://kidshealth.org

Nemours, established in 1936 by philanthropist Alfred I. duPont, is dedicated to improving the health and spirit of children. Nemours also creates high-impact educational projects that positively affect the health of children. These projects are developed through the Nemours Center for Children's Health Media, a division of Nemours dedicated to this task. The center creates award-winning, family-friendly health information in a number of formats, including print, video, and online. Its KidsHealth and TeensHealth websites include sections on coping with divorce.

For Further Reading

Books

Andrew J. Cherlin, *The Marriage-Go-Round: The State of Marriage and the Family in America Today.* New York: Alfred A. Knopf, 2009.

Phyllis Chester, *Mothers on Trial: The Battle for Children and Custody.* Chicago: Lawrence Hill Books, 2011.

James G. Dwyer, *The Relationship Rights of Children.* New York: Cambridge University Press, 2006.

Joseph Goldstein, Anna Freud, and Albert J. Solnit, *Beyond the Best Interests of the Child.* New York: Free Press, 1979.

Elizabeth Marquardt, *Between Two Worlds: The Inner Lives of Children of Divorce.* New York: Crown Publishers, 2005.

Mary Ann Mason, *From Father's Property to Children's Rights: The History of Child Custody in the United States.* New York: Columbia University Press, 1994.

Mary Ann Mason, *The Custody Wars: Why Children Are Losing the Legal Battle and What We Can Do About It.* New York: Basic Books, 1999.

David Popenoe, *Families Without Fathers: Fathers, Marriage, and Children in American Society.* New Brunswick, NJ: Transaction Publishers, 2009.

Andrew Root, *The Children of Divorce: The Loss of Family as the Loss of Being.* Grand Rapids, MI: Brazos, 2010.

Philip M. Stahl, *Conducting Child Custody Evaluations: From Basic to Complex Issues.* Thousand Oaks, CA: Sage, 2011.

Trudi Strain Trueit, *Surviving Divorce: Teens Talk About What Hurts and What Helps.* New York: Franklin Watts, 2007.

Periodicals

Matt Carver, "Child Custody Considerations on School Grounds," *School Administrator,* August 2011.

Andrea Corn and Howard Raab, "Age-Appropriate Time Sharing for Divorced Parents," *Florida Bar Journal,* June 2007.

Cynthia Dizicks and Kristen Mack, "Divorcing Couple War over Child's Religion," *Chicago Tribune,* February 16, 2010.

James Wilson Douglas, "The Grandkids and Your Rights: Understanding Your Role in Custody and Visitation," *Family Advocate,* Summer 2008.

FindLaw, "Various Types of Custody," www.findlaw.com.

Scott A. Lerner, "'Standard Visitation' and the Best Interest of the Child," *Illinois Bar Journal,* March 2009.

Dahlia Lithwick, "Rethinking Fathers' Rights," *Newsweek,* August 25, 2008.

Ken MacQueen, "Years Later, the Girl Found a Drawer Full of Plane Tickets the Father She'd Been Told Had Never Wanted to See Her Had Sent," *Maclean's,* June 16, 2008.

Douglass Mossman and Christian G. Weston, "Divorce, Custody, and Parental Consent for Psychiatric Treatment," *Current Psychology,* August 2008.

Margaret S. Price, "Divorce Issues and the Special Needs Child," *American Journal of Family Law,* Spring 2011.

Ellen Weber, "Is There a Favorite Parent?," Psychologytoday .com, March 29, 2010.

Wisconsin Law Journal, "Commentary: 'Best Interests' Hard to Define," July 5, 2010.

Index